Digital
Command Control

2ND EDITION

Ian Morton

Ian Allan
PUBLISHING

Aspects of Modelling: Digital Command Control 2nd edition
Ian Morton

First published 2007
Reprinted 2007 and 2008
This Second Edition 2010

ISBN 978 0 7110 3499 0

Published by Ian Allan Publishing

an imprint of Ian Allan Publishing Ltd, Hersham, Surrey KT12 4RG.
Printed in England by Ian Allan Printing Ltd, Hersham, Surrey KT12 4RG.

Visit the Ian Allan Publishing website at www.ianallanpublishing.com

Distributed in the United States of America and Canada by BookMasters
Distribution Services.

Contents

Foreword 4

Foreword to the Second edition 4

CHAPTER 1 **An introduction to DCC** 5
The Myths and Misconceptions
So where did DCC come from?

CHAPTER 2 **Converting to DCC** 10
Making the change, The next Step
Something to avoid

CHAPTER 3 **Command stations, boosters and cabs** 14
Multiple Controllers

CHAPTER 4 **Locomotive Decoders** 22

CHAPTER 5 **Accessory Decoders** 57

CHAPTER 6 **Wiring for DCC** 61
Power districts

CHAPTER 7 **First Use** 67

CHAPTER 8 **Advanced Use** 70
Tailoring decoder performance
Double heading

Glossary 78

Trouble-shooting Guide 79

Manufacturers and Suppliers (UK) 80

Foreword

Digital Command Control has generated much discussion and comment amongst railway modellers. You will find people who are passionately in favour of it and others so vehemently opposed to it that you would think it had been invented by Dr Beeching himself. Much of the debate has taken place without the benefit of facts or evidence and in this respect I hope that this volume can at least shed a little light on the proceedings.

Whilst I have no axe to grind either for or against DCC, I have observed its development, and that of many of the command control systems that preceded it. The current debate has all the hallmarks of the two-rail versus three-rail arguments of the 1950s and, I suspect, the clockwork versus electric confrontation from even further back.

Everyone needs to make up their own mind about DCC. For those with a large layout or massive collection of locomotives the cost of conversion may seem too high. For those with more modest aspirations the same may also seem true. For those just entering, or coming back to, the hobby the choice is much easier. It all comes down to the question of what DCC can do for you.

For a young child's train set a simple DCC system, such as Bachmann's E-Z Command controller, can make connecting up and operation easier than ever before. For a single engine shunting layout it would be far more a matter of personal choice.

Scale and gauge are not bars to using DCC. Locomotives from Z through to Gauge 1 and above have successfully been fitted with decoders and just about every possible variation of 4mm scale has been DCC equipped from P4 to 009.

Despite what many of its opponents may say, in most cases a DCC layout is easier to wire up than an equivalent conventional layout and DCC equipped locomotives normally perform better than the same locomotive on conventional control. On the other hand some people will never need the extra functionality that DCC offers. But, once you have read the contents of this book at least you will have the information to make the decision about whether DCC is right for you and, if it is, how to select and install the system that best meets your needs.

I should add that the use of a model railway in these pages to illustrate an idea does not imply that the layout shown is DCC operated. The pictures have been chosen to explain what DCC can do for you. Finally I should like to thank those who have provided photographs and information, and my family for letting me spend so many uninterrupted hours bashing away at the computer keyboard.

Happy modelling.

Ian Morton

Foreword to the Second Edition

In the three and a half years since I wrote the original text DCC has become less of a novelty, although it is still capable of arousing passionate arguments both for and against. It is now possible to buy ready-to-run locomotives fitted with DCC decoders, DCC operated lights and even ones with sound. I have revised much of the text to take account of changes and developments in the DCC marketplace. I have removed some of the more advanced content and this will feature in a new book that is in preparation.

An introduction to DCC

When operating a model railway most people want to feel that they are driving a locomotive.

On a conventional model railway, if you want to have more than one locomotive on the track at any one time then you need to provide isolated track sections to store the locomotives that you are not using so that they don't move when you turn the controller on. If you wish to operate more than one locomotive at a time it starts to get complicated as you now need a controller for each locomotive, connected to electrically separate sections of track. You also need to be able to select which sections of track are connected to each controller.

Even on a simple layout the wiring involved with multiple controllers, section switches and isolating switches can become complex and confusing. Of course once you have installed and sorted out any problems with the wiring you then have to learn how to operate it all.

Despite all the time, effort and expense involved in setting your conventional control system up you will still find that before you can drive the train you will have to do a lot of work switching the track power. Common railway activities like double-heading, banking or parking engines next to each other are all difficult to achieve due to the inflexibility of the system.

For years modellers have put up with these limitations or created involved methods to get around them but now there is a better way. The computer 'chip' has invaded every area of life and model railways are no exception.

The technology is called Digital Command Control, normally abbreviated to DCC. Using this technology it is possible to run as many locomotives as you wish on your layout without having to worry about selecting which track is connected to which controller or worrying about where the isolated sections are to park your locomotive. All you need to do is choose a locomotive and drive it.

Even better, the system is simple to install and operate; it requires less technical knowledge than wiring up a conventional system.

Despite this there are many myths and misconceptions surrounding DCC. Once you actually take the plunge you will find that there is nothing to be scared of.

The Myths and Misconceptions

It's expensive.
Well, yes it is if you are trying to convert a medium or large layout and matching locomotive stud all at once. It would be far better to phase DCC operation in or, if you really must do it all at once, save up for it.

The decoders are difficult to fit.
They can be. Small locomotives, such as 'N' scale saddle-tanks can be difficult. Vintage commercial products with live metal chassis can also cause problems, as can kit and scratchbuilt steam locomotives but in many cases there is a workaround. There are very few models where it really is impossible to fit a DCC decoder.

DCC won't work with certain types of point.
Simply not true. DCC is more sensitive to short circuits so if you have a problem with incorrectly wired or built points or wildly out of gauge wheelsets that cause a short going over pointwork then DCC will highlight the problem. The fault lies with your wiring or wheels and ought to be corrected anyway.

Even on medium-sized layouts the control panel can be intimidating when you use conventional analogue control.

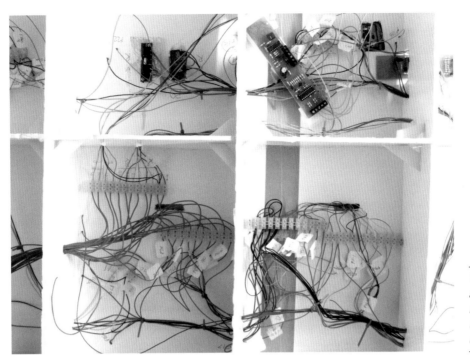

With conventional analogue control the number of wires underneath a layout can be frightening.

DCC needs special wiring.

Not true. Whilst you may wish to put special wiring in you can replace a conventional controller on your layout with a DCC one and it will work as long as you don't have any high frequency track cleaners or lighting installed.

DCC needs programming.

Programming is a bad choice of word. As a minimum all you need to do is set the decoder's number in each locomotive. This is usually a matter of a few key presses. That's it. You don't need to know, adjust or program anything else. Setting a video recorder is harder.

DCC isn't needed on a small layout.

DCC is well suited to small layouts. The ability to stop a locomotive anywhere, regardless of dead sections, is a boon to operators of compact layouts. If you had a small layout depicting a motive power depot you could park locomotives nose to tail in prototypical fashion. You could also operate the points and signals from your handheld controller rather than a control panel.

DCC isn't needed on a large layout.

DCC is ideally suited to large layouts too. The ability to select any locomotive and then run it without having to worry about setting section switches, reverse loops and isolating sections means that you can concentrate on driving the train.

You need to buy a special tester.

Like most technological gadgets offered to consumers, DCC items work when you take them out of the box. In the unlikely event that they don't – take them back to the retailer.

You need a computer to get the best out of DCC.

You can link DCC up to a computer if you wish. The computer can work some, or all, of your layout if you do, but you don't have to.

It's confusing.

That's what this book is for. The ideas behind DCC are simple and you don't need to know exactly how it works in order to use it, just like you don't need to know how an internal combustion engine works in order to drive a car.

So where did DCC come from?

Well, the idea has been around since the 1940s but it was only in the 1970s that 'multiple train control' systems started to become commercially feasible. There were a number of false starts and equipment from competing manufacturers was not compatible meaning that once you selected one of these expensive systems you were limited to what that manufacturer offered. The early systems were not very reliable and there was limited take-up so they disappeared from the general market. However, the idea lived on. The National Model Railroad Association (NMRA) in America adopted a proposal for a set of standards for multiple train control from Lenz in Germany. They believed that if all the equipment was compatible it would benefit both manufacturers and modellers. The standards were developed; the system named DCC and made freely available for manufacturers to use. Now there are a wide range of manufacturers offering all sorts of DCC equipment. You can even buy DCC train sets from Bachmann and Hornby in the UK.

Whilst you don't need to know how DCC works in order to use it many people are curious. If you really don't want to know how it works its magic, feel free to skip on to the next chapter.

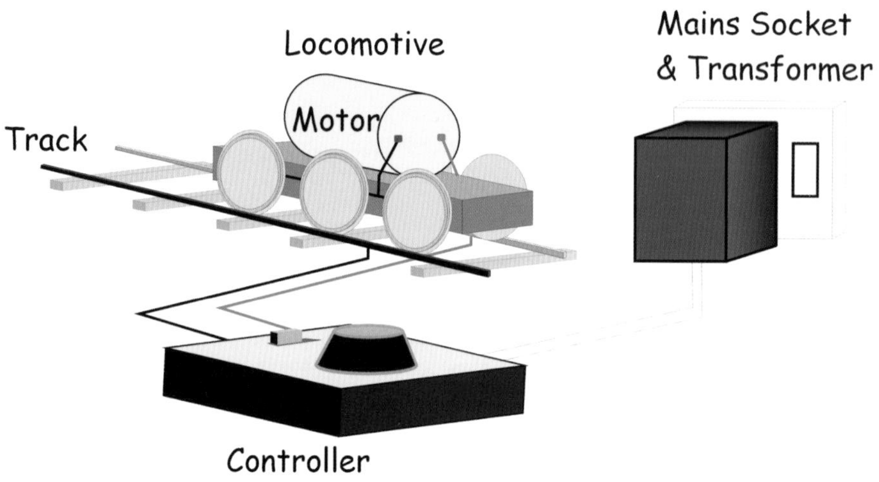

This diagram shows the electrical connections needed to make a model locomotive move. A transformer is plugged into a mains socket. The transformer converts the mains voltage electricity into something safer for us to use. The transformer powers the controller which has a knob to control the locomotive's speed and a switch to control its direction. Two wires from the controller run to the rails, one each side of the track. The locomotive has metal wheels that pick up electricity from the track and they, in turn, are connected to the locomotive's motor.

Inside each locomotive, on a conventional analogue layout, is an electric motor connected to the track. A standard model railway controller is also connected to the track. As we turn the knob on the controller from OFF to MAXIMUM the motor in the locomotive will run faster and faster. When we turn the knob back to OFF the motor stops. If we then change the direction switch and move the knob again the motor runs in the opposite direction. This allows us to control the direction and speed of our model, but how does the magic actually work?

Each of the rails is connected to the controller. The wheels of the locomotive are electrically connected to the motor. With the locomotive standing on the track the controller is connected via the rails and wheels to the motor.

The controller puts a VOLTAGE across the two rails. This is what causes the motor to run. As the voltage increases from 0 (OFF) to 12 Volts (MAXIMUM) the motor goes faster. If we change the direction switch then the voltage is applied the other way around and goes from 0 (OFF) to -12 Volts (MAXIMUM – in reverse).

If we want to have more than one locomotive on the layout then the other locomotives must be parked on lengths of track that are not connected to the controller. When we want to use a different locomotive then the track that it is on must be connected to the controller, and the other track disconnected. A track or locomotive that is disconnected from the controller is called 'isolated'.

On a simple layout you can use the points to isolate locomotives. Most commercially produced points isolate one track and power the other – the one on the direction that the point is set but for more complex layouts or operation you will find that some lengths of track need to be isolated by means of switches on a

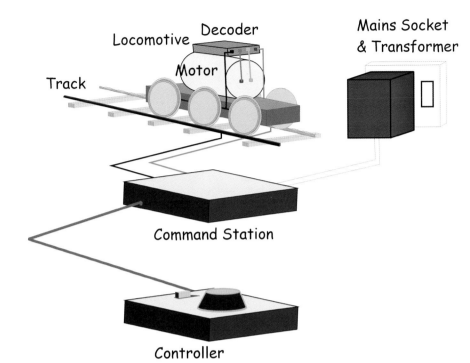

With a DCC system there are two extra items, a command station and a decoder. You can plug a number of controllers into a command station and run as many locomotives as you like on the same length of track. Each locomotive needs to have its own decoder which responds to the signals sent by the command station.

control panel. Similarly if you have two or more controllers, so that you can have more than one locomotive moving at a time, you will find that there is a need for control panel switches to choose which controller is connected to a particular track.

On a medium to large layout these extra isolated sections and switches lead to a lot of wiring. Whilst the individual circuits are simple the sheer number of switches and wires can make the underside of a layout look like a complex jumble of cables.

A DCC system still uses the rails to carry electricity to the locomotives but works differently. DCC track not only carries the electricity but also information, in the form of electrical signals, that is used to control the locomotives. Each locomotive is fitted with an electronic circuit called a decoder that reads the signals and responds accordingly. The DCC command station supplies the power and creates the signals used to control the locomotives. With DCC you do not need to isolate spare locomotives and you can, depending on your layout and reactions, run more than one locomotive using a single controller.

Converting to DCC

DCC is suitable for all kinds of layouts. John de Frayssinet's OO9 masterpiece 'County Gate' is a DCC layout and is fully automated using Digitrax controllers.

There are many things to think about when deciding which system is best for you, and these will vary depending on your particular situation. For example, it is a lot easier to choose DCC if you are starting afresh than if you have a large collection of DC locomotives that will need to be converted. Remember, each locomotive needs its own decoder and some people will choose to have these fitted for them. If you intend to convert a large collection of locomotives, the cost could be prohibitive. It can be difficult to fit decoders in some locomotives, especially small ones – even DCC-ready ones can prove tricky at times.

Conventional DC operation has advantages if you are using older ready-to-run stock, kit-built locomotives or small models such as 'N' and 'OO9' as you don't need to find extra space for a decoder and just about any ready-to-run or kit-built locomotive that you will encounter can be run without any modification. If you only ever need to have one or two locomotives on the layout then the wiring will be simple; however as a layout increases in complexity the need for switches and wires increases rapidly and can result in control panels that have more switches and indicator lights than the average power station.

DCC operation comes into its own on layouts with a number of locomotives. Operation is no longer constrained by the location of electrical sections – you can park locomotives anywhere and operate trains just like the real railways. For example, at a steam-age terminus the locomotive that brought the train in would follow the departing coaches out to the end of the platform so that the signalman wouldn't forget about it. This is easy to replicate with DCC without worrying about switches or electrical sections.

With DCC the decoder in each locomotive can be configured to get the best possible performance out of the locomotive. By configuring the decoder you can set the starting voltage, maximum speed, acceleration rate and many other things. This means that your shunter can have a lower top speed than your express passenger locomotive and that the express will accelerate more quickly than the heavy freight.

Most DCC decoders come with the ability to operate extra functions, such as lights. You can even buy ones that mimic the sounds made by real locomotives. All these features add to the price and complexity of a model, but provide possibilities that are difficult to implement with conventional DC.

Apart from the locomotives there is also the matter of points and accessories to consider. Point motors and other powered accessories can be operated conventionally using switches on the control panel, or from a DCC controller using special decoders. It is perfectly possible to use DCC for the locomotives and conventional control for the accessories, or even vice versa. If you opt for DCC control then you need to purchase special decoders which are mounted under the baseboard; these are then connected to the DCC controller and the accessories being controlled.

The advantage of DCC control of your accessories is that it can be done from your DCC controller, which is very convenient if you have a handheld controller and follow your train around the layout, or from a computer. The computer display shows a diagram of the layout and you click the mouse on points to change them. Apart from saving the effort and expense of building a physical control panel it is also easy to modify the display if your layout changes or to add automation to certain areas, such as the fiddle yard or a branch line.

The downside of DCC control of accessories is that if you don't use a computer it is impossible to stop two operators setting up conflicting routes and the decoders are relatively expensive, typically costing £8 per point motor controlled.

Making the Change

I would not recommend converting one controller on a layout to a DCC Command Station and leaving the others as ordinary analogue controllers. Whilst some people suggest this as one way to convert a layout to DCC in stages it suffers from a number of potential pitfalls. Firstly if a locomotive bridges the gap between DCC and DC controlled sections then the AC track voltage can cause damage to electronic components in transistorised controllers. Similarly the DC voltage can cause unexpected results in the DCC controlled area. Secondly the widespread use of common return on analogue circuits can lead to the AC and DC voltages appearing in places where they ought not to be. Finally systems that superimpose a high frequency AC voltage on the analogue DC voltage, such as constant coach lighting systems and high-frequency track cleaners, like those produced by Relco, will disrupt, and quite possibly damage, the DCC system.

It is quite possible to fit decoders to your locomotives and still operate them on conventional DC. This approach would allow you to build up a selection of DCC fitted locomotives before changing the controller(s) over. Whilst it is possible to operate locomotives without decoders on some DCC systems it cannot be recommended as it is easy to damage or destroy motors doing this.

DCC decoders have the ability to operate on analogue DC layouts. This enables you to fit decoders to your locomotives as time and funds allow before switching over to DCC. You will probably want to set up a small DCC test track with a Command Station so that you can test the decoder installation in each locomotive, set the decoder parameters and get used to operating the system. Meanwhile your layout will continue to work just the way that it did before. There are a small number of possible pitfalls to watch out for.

The analogue (DC) mode can be disabled on any decoder. This setting is found in CV29 (see *Chapter 8 Advanced Use* for more details). If the locomotive is happy on the DCC test track but will not respond on the layout then you need to turn the analogue mode on.

Ensure that there is a brief spell of zero voltage on the track when you change direction on the controller. If your controller does not do this then it is quite possible that decoder-equipped locomotives will not recognise the change of direction and either continue travelling in the same direction or stop dead.

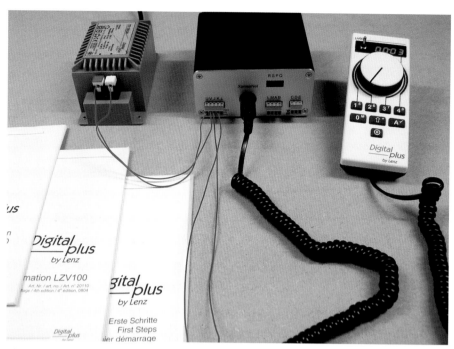

You will need a DCC controller to test locomotives that have had a DCC decoder installed, even if you haven't converted your layout to DCC yet. This is a Lenz LH90 handset, LZV100 control station and TR150 transformer.

The easiest way to establish if this is a problem is to try it and see. Get a decoder-equipped locomotive up to about half speed and flick the direction switch. If the locomotive changes direction (hopefully by slowing down to a stop first and then accelerating again) all is well. Otherwise you will need to add a separate direction switch on the output of the controller. This should be a Double Pole Double Throw Centre-Off Switch with Break Before Make contacts. The switch should be wired as shown in the diagram below and used INSTEAD of the one on the controller. Placing some tape over the controller's switch will stop it being used by accident. These switches are available from most electronic component suppliers. Purchasing a switch with a centre off position allows you to disconnect the controller totally from the track and ensures that you must go through a zero voltage state when changing direction. Three suggested suppliers are listed below.

Maplin Electronics Ltd.	*part no.*	*JK30H 10A Toggle DPDT F*
Rapid Electronics Ltd.	*part no.*	*75-0145 DPDT Centre-off*
Squires Model & Craft Tools	*part no.*	*STT200 Standard Toggle DPDT C/Off On-Off-On*

How to wire a reversing switch between the controller and the track.

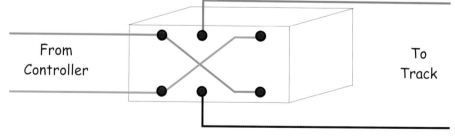

From
Controller

To
Track

DPDT Switch
(From underneath)

If your analogue controllers produce pulsed power (for example half-wave rectification, pulse width modulation) then decoder equipped locomotives will sometimes run erratically. To solve this you will need to connect two capacitors across the output of each analogue controller as shown in the diagram below. These capacitors are available from most electronic component suppliers. Three suggested suppliers are listed below.

Maplin Electronics Ltd.	*part no.*	*AT24B AxlElect 4700µF 35V*
Rapid Electronics Ltd.	*part no.*	*11-1418 4700µF 35V radial electrolytic capacitor*
Squires Model & Craft Tools	*part no.*	*541-193 35V 4700µF capacitor*

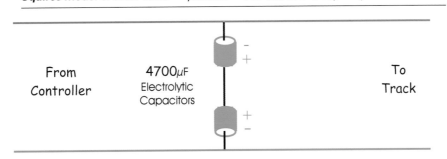

From
Controller

4700µF
Electrolytic
Capacitors

To
Track

How to convert pulsed power DC for use when running DCC decoder-fitted locomotives from an analogue (DC) controller. The capacitors smooth the pulsed output providing a constant DC voltage.

The Next Step

As well as fitting decoders to your locomotives you should also consider working on the layout wiring ready for the changeover. Identify any extra track feeds or section gaps that will be needed and install them ready for use. Ideally every piece of rail should be connected to a wire, do not rely on fishplates for electrical connections.

Reversing loops, turntables and wyes will also need to be considered. Just as with analogue control there are various ways to arrange these on a DCC system (see Chapter 6 *Wiring for DCC*).

Once you are ready to turn on the DCC system you will need to disconnect the old analogue controllers and section switches. The tracks should be connected to the track bus (see Chapter 6 *Wiring for DCC*) and the DCC controllers connected up. Finally, remove the locomotives that don't have decoders fitted from the track and switch on.

Something to Avoid

Depending on your layout you might be tempted to try to combine analogue and DCC controllers, for example using DCC on the branch line and the existing analogue controllers on the main line. Whilst it is technically possible to do this it does run the risk of damaging both control systems as well as the locomotives.

Firstly the analogue and DCC sections of the layout need to be completely electrically isolated. You cannot get the systems to work together if you have used common return wiring. More importantly when a locomotive bridges the gap between the two sections the DCC track voltage can flow into the analogue section of the layout. This can cause a voltage difference of over 20V to appear on the track. Many motors and analogue controllers will not take kindly to this kind of abuse.

CHAPTER 3

Command stations, boosters and cabs

DCC controllers come in a wide variety of designs. The Bachmann Dynamis handset has a graphical display screen and has no wires connecting it to the layout. Instead it uses an infra-red link to the command station.

The control side of DCC systems consists of three building blocks. Depending on the system that you buy one or more of them may be in the same box.

The cab is the item that allows you to control the speed and direction of one or more locomotives. Some cabs use knobs, some have buttons and those manufactured by NCE have both! Depending on the system, the cab may also be able to control a number of locomotive functions, such as lights and sound, change points and set locomotive decoder settings. A layout may have a number of cabs so that a number of people can run trains at the same time.

The command station is the brains of the system. It takes information from the cabs and converts it into DCC format. A layout only needs one command station. If you try to install more than one then they will send conflicting DCC signals along the track and nothing will work.

The booster is the brawn to the command station's brains. It takes the weak DCC signal and amplifies it so that it is powerful enough to power locomotives and accessories. Large layouts and those where a large number of locomotives or accessories will be in use will need a number of boosters in order to provide sufficient power.

There are DCC systems to suit most requirements from a child's train set through to a complex multi-operator empire. Selecting a suitable system is a matter of matching the facilities offered to your requirements and budget. Whilst you can operate any DCC decoder with any DCC command station, the cabs, command stations and boosters are not necessarily compatible between manufacturers.

By and large, the more flexibility and functionality that you require from your DCC system, the more that you will have to pay. Fortunately in many cases it is possible to add extra units to a basic system to expand it without having to discard your original items.

At the bottom end of the range of price and functionality are the simple systems, such as the Bachmann E-Z Command which have limited capability but are exceedingly simple to install and operate. At the top end of the range are systems which allow more cabs and boosters than you are ever likely to need, can be interfaced to a computer as well as operating many functions and accessories. In between these extremes are some mid-range systems that have sufficient functionality and flexibility for most British layouts.

Many of the DCC manufacturers and retailers have displays at the major model railway exhibitions and if you are considering an expensive system then you would be well advised to go along and try it for yourself. However good a system appears on paper there are a number of questions that can only be answered when you can see the system in reality.

- If it is a walkaround, does the cab fit comfortably in your hand?
- Is the speed control easy to operate?
- Are the buttons large enough for you to operate comfortably?
- Can you read the display?

I have included a table of most of the DCC starter sets available on the UK market at the time of writing (late 2009). Bear in mind that the DCC market changes rapidly and new units appear, features are added and updated on a regular basis so please use it only as a guide rather than the final arbiter in your decision.

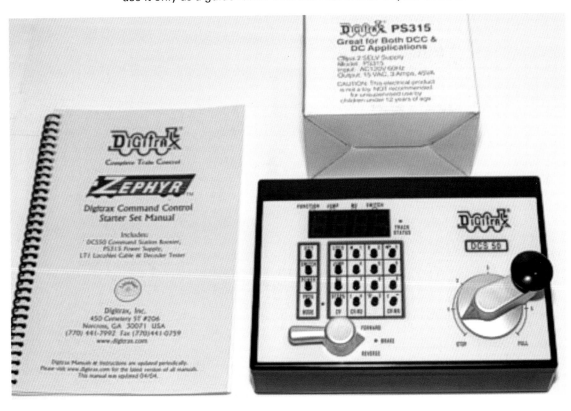

Digitrax's Zephyr has controls that are more like a diesel locomotive's than a computer's.

The key questions that you need to ask yourself are as follows –

How many locomotives am I likely to have?

If you only have room for eight locomotives on your layout, then even if you own eighty you can get by with a system that has 9 locomotive addresses. If you are installing DCC on a club layout with a vast pool of locomotives then you may need the ability to use over 1000 addresses.

How many locomotives will be running at once?

The more locomotives that are running at once, the more power you need. Don't forget that with DCC you can operate several locomotives at once. For example you could have two trains looping the main line, one double-headed, whilst you shunt the yard. That would be four locomotives just on one cab.

Will I be using carriage lighting?

The constant voltage on the track makes it easy to install things like carriage lighting – but all those lights take current. This needs to be added on to your power requirement.

How many cabs do I need?

Each operator will need their own cab. You may also want some extras to save switching between different locomotives in use at the same time.

Do I want walkaround control?

Many DCC systems have both fixed and walkaround cabs available. In the past most UK layouts have used fixed control systems where the operator sits in one location with all the necessary controls to hand.

With walkaround cabs the operators can move around with their trains. Obviously this means that any controls must be situated near to where they are used but as DCC removes the need for block and power switches you only need to consider controls for points, signals and other accessories. Of course if you use DCC to control these items as well then everything can be operated from the walkaround cab. It is, of course, possible to have a combination of fixed and walkaround cabs if you wish.

Walkaround cabs come in two varieties, tethered and remote control. Tethered cabs are connected to the layout by a long cable. You plug these into sockets placed around the layout. You can unplug the cab and move it to a different socket without having to stop the train. Remote control cabs use radio or infra-red signals to link to a receiver situated under the layout. These are more expensive and less common than the tethered variety.

With controllers of this type there is a trade-off between number of controls and functionality. If there are a few buttons then it is easy to perform simple operations but can be difficult, or even impossible to do more complex tasks. If there are a lot of buttons then it requires fewer key presses to do complex tasks but it is easier to get the wrong button when you are watching the train rather than looking at the controller.

Is there a cab bus?

Many DCC systems have a system that allows extra cabs, boosters and other accessories to be connected together easily. This is normally called a cab, or control, bus. Where a common standard is used equipment such as cabs from different manufacturers can be used together.

Two common cab buses are the Lenz XpressNet (also called XBus III) and the Digitrax Loconet. The two systems are not compatible with each other but any XpressNet compatible item can, in theory, be plugged into, and used with, an XpressNet bus regardless of the manufacturer. Similarly any LocoNet compatible item can be used on a LocoNet bus. If the manufacturer of your chosen DCC system has their own type of cab bus then you will be restricted to using only their cabs, boosters and accessories.

Do I want to operate points and signals?

You can use DCC to run locomotives but stick to conventional systems to operate points and signals, or you can use DCC for those too. You can even use DCC for the points and conventional control for the locomotives if you wish, probably as an interim measure whilst you fit your locomotives with decoders.

Do I want a computer interface?

A computer can drive trains whilst you act as signalman, can be the signalman whilst you drive trains or can drive trains at the same time that you do, providing other traffic for you to work around.

Is there a means of updating the command station's program?

Some systems have a facility to download updated software from the internet, some by replacing one of the integrated circuits inside the controller, some require that the unit be returned to the manufacturer for upgrading and the rest have no upgrade path.

An upgraded program may be needed to solve problems with the way that the command station behaves or to provide new functions.

Do I have any special track formations?

Wyes, reversing loops and turntables all need special treatment. Do you want to operate the voltage changeover manually or automatically?

How many functions do I need on my locomotives?

Modern light systems can take up four decoder outputs. Then there is sound, remote uncoupling, smoke generators....

Can I install it all at once or do I want to do it in stages?

Features like a computer interface or automatically operated reversing loops can be added later. Point and signal operation could be converted to DCC once the locomotive conversion is complete.

How much can I afford?

Be realistic. It is easy to get carried away with features that you may never need or use.

Starter Set Comparison

Unit	Bachmann E-Z Command	Hornby Select	Hornby Elite	MRC/Gaugemaster Prodigy Advance2
Speed control	Knob	Knob	Knob (two throttles in one case)	Knob
Maximum number of extra controllers	At least 2	None	8 – Hornby Select only	Up to 99
Locomotive addresses stored in controller ("stack")	0	0	254	25
Locomotive address range	1-9	1-59	1-9999 – Extra controllers can only access 59	1-9999
Ability to name locomotives	No	No	Yes. Names are not available on extra controllers	No
Speed steps	28	14, 28 or 128	14, 28 or 128	14, 28 or 128
Maximum Current	1A	1A	3A	3.5A
Additional Power Boosters	Optional 5A booster	No	No	No
Accessory control (points, etc.)	No	Yes (40 items)	Yes	Yes
Route control	No	No	No	Up to 32 routes each operating up to 8 accessories
Consists	No	Universal	Universal	Advanced & Universal
Other expansion	Lenz X-bus for additional controllers (E-Z Command Companion only)	Can be used as an extra controller with a Hornby Elite	XpressNet for additional controllers (Hornby Select only). USB port for downloading software updates and limited computer interface.	MRC Throttle Bus
Reversing Loop Capability	Extra module available	Extra module available	Extra module available	Extra module available
Number of functions	9 (F0 – F8)	9 (F0 – F7)	13 (F0 – F12)	28
Programming capability	Decoder address only	Locomotive address only	Yes	Yes
Programming on the main	All other locomotives must be removed from layout	All other locomotives must be removed from layout	Yes	Yes
Walkaround controller	No	No	No	Yes
Analogue locomotive operation	Yes	Yes	Yes	No
Power Supply	Included	Included	Included	Included

Unit	Lenz Start Set 90	Lenz Start Set 100	NCE PowerCab	NCE PowerPro
Speed control	Knob	Button	Buttons and thumb wheel	Buttons and thumb wheel
Maximum number of extra controllers	31	31	1 (more if upgraded to PowerPro)	62
Locomotive addresses stored in controller ("stack")	8	8	9999	9999
Locomotive address range	9999	9999	9999	9999
Ability to name locomotives	No	No		
Speed steps	14, 27, 28, 128	14, 27, 28, 128	14,28,128	14,28,128
Maximum Current	Up to 5A	Up to 5A	2A	5A
Additional Power Boosters	Yes	Yes	Yes	Yes
Accessory control (points, etc.)	Yes	Yes	Yes	Yes
Route control	No	No	Yes. 256 routes with up to 10 items per route.	Yes. 256 routes with up to 10 items per route.
Consists	Universal/Advanced	Universal/Advanced	Universal/Advanced	Universal/Advanced
Other expansion	Lenz XpressNet	Lenz XpressNet	NCE Cab Bus. Optional computer interface	NCE Cab Bus. Optional computer interface..
Reversing Loop Capability	Extra module available	Extra module available	Extra module available	Extra module available
Number of functions	13 (F0 – F12)	13 (F0 – F12)	13 (F0 – F12)	13 (F0 – F12)
Programming capability	Yes	Yes	Yes	Yes
Programming on the main	Yes	Yes	All other locomotives must be removed from layout	Yes
Walkaround controller	Yes	Yes	Yes	Yes
Analogue locomotive operation	Yes	Yes	No	No
Power Supply	Not included	Not included	Included	Not Included

Unit	Digitrax Zephyr	Digitrax Super Chief	Bachmann Dynamis
Speed control	Regulator lever	Knob (two throttles in one case)	Joystick
Maximum number of extra controllers	10	119	None. 3 with ProBox upgrade.
Locomotive addresses stored in controller ("stack")	0	0	40 – System can only remember names and settings for 40 locomotives.
Locomotive address range	9000	9000	1-9999
Ability to name locomotives	No	No	Yes, up to 16 characters. The same names are used by extra controllers.
Speed steps	14,28,128	128	14,28,128
Maximum Current	2.5A	5A	2.5A
Additional Power Boosters	Yes	Yes	Optional 5A booster
Accessory control (points, etc.)	Yes	Yes	Yes
Route control	No	Yes. 32 routes of up to 8 items.	No.
Consists	Universal	Universal/Advanced	Universal and Advanced
Other expansion	LocoNet	LocoNet	ECOSLink interface
Reversing Loop Capability	Extra module available	Extra module available	Currently, no
Number of functions	9 (F0 – F8)	29 (F0 – F28)	21 (F0 – F20)
Programming capability	Yes	Yes	Yes – on main. On programming track with Pro Box upgrade
Programming on the main	Yes	Yes	All other locomotives must be removed from layout unless the Pro Box upgrade is installed.
Walkaround controller	No	Yes	Yes
Analogue locomotive operation	Yes	Yes	No
Power Supply	Included	Included	Included

Multiple Controllers

Unlike conventional DC layouts where you can mix controllers from different manufacturers when you use DCC your choice of controllers to work with a specific DCC system is more limited. This is in direct contrast to the situation with locomotive and accessory decoders where, to be NMRA compatible, the decoders must be able to work with any DCC controller. The reason is that whilst the controller output and decoder input is specified in detail by NMRA (National Model Railroad Association) standards, the actual operation and connection of controllers is not.

The various DCC manufacturers have approached the situation in a number of ways. Lenz have a system for connecting extra controllers called XpressNet (formerly called X-Bus) which is also used by some other manufacturers, such as Hornby. Digitrax have a different system called LocoNet and most other manufacturers restrict you to using their own products.

Setting up Hornby Controllers on an XpressNet

Whilst the cab bus systems are all different, the procedure for setting any of them up is similar. As an example I shall show how to connect a Hornby Elite to a number of Hornby Select controllers.

The Hornby Elite and Select come with XpressNet connections that allow up to seven Select controllers to be plugged in to an Elite or Select controller that is acting as the command station. Whilst the Hornby Elite has two control knobs the fact that they share a keypad means that it is better suited to allowing one person to have direct control of two trains rather than two people to use it simultaneously. For much of the time this is not a problem as many people often run trains on their own. However it is nice to be able to have a second controller so that a visitor can run trains, for use at a station some distance from the main controller, as a walkaround controller so that you aren't tied to the main control panel or even for use on the workbench. Given that Hornby Select controllers can be obtained on the secondhand market and new from retailers who split up train sets, extra controllers can be obtained quite cheaply, buying a Select as a second controller can seem a good idea, so how does it work in practice?

The Hornby Select comes in two forms, the R8213 Select Digital Control which comes with a power pack and the R8235 Select Walkabout which doesn't. At retail price the R8235 Walkabout is £18.49 cheaper, but in practice the R8213 with a power pack is more widely available at a lower price. This actually works to our benefit as it enables the Select to be used as a standalone controller on the workbench or as an extra controller on the layout.

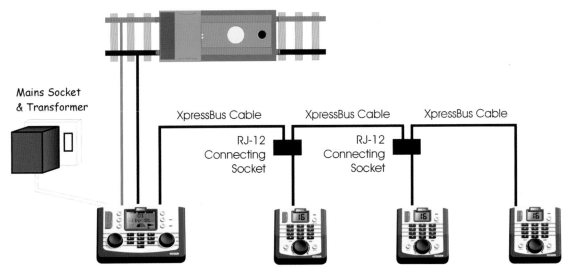

Mains Socket & Transformer

XpressBus Cable   XpressBus Cable   XpressBus Cable

RJ-12 Connecting Socket   RJ-12 Connecting Socket

Daisy-chaining controllers. The Elite controller on the left is connected to the power supply and the track and acts as the main controller. The Select controllers are linked to the Elite by 4-wire cables in a daisy chain. The Select controllers are not connected to the track or the power supply.

To connect the two controllers you need a special lead. These are available from Hornby as R8266 DCC RJ-12 4-wire 3M lead. If you want to connect more than one extra controllers these can be 'daisy-chained'. As Hornby uses the XpressNet system you can purchase leads and extra sockets from any Lenz compatible range.

No matter how many controllers you connect together on the XpressNet only one is plugged into the power supply and connected to the track. This is the master controller and does all the clever stuff of sending out the DCC signals to the locomotive and accessory decoders, gathering information from the extra controllers and generally keeping the system running. If you have more than one extra controller, each of the extra controllers needs to have a number to identify it, so that the master controller knows which one it is talking to.

Setting up the XpressBus

The first time that you plug the controllers in you will need to set them up. This is a simple process that will only take a few seconds.

1. Plug the master controller in and turn it on.
2. Insert an XpressBus cable into one of the XpressBus sockets on the master controller.
3. Plug the other end of the cable into the first of the extra controllers. If you are going to have more than one extra controller then you need to plug the cable into an RJ12 Connecting Socket and plug the socket into the extra controller.
4. The extra controller will power up and show 'HC' on its display.

If you only have one extra controller your system is now ready to use.
If you have more than one extra controller you need to continue with step 5.

5. Press 'Select' on the extra controller and enter a controller number between 1 and 31, the best idea is to start at 1 and work your way up. Then press 'Select' again.
6. Plug an XpressBus cable into the other XpressBus socket on the RJ12 connecting socket then return to step 3.

Repeat steps 4 to 6 until all the controllers are plugged in.

In future when you turn the main controller on all the extra controllers will power up at the same time.

Operating with Multiple Controllers

To run a train with one of the extra controllers simply enter its address on the keyboard and press 'Select'. The locomotive is now under your control. Remember that, unlike the Elite, the Select can only operate locomotives with addresses between 1 and 59 and doesn't have the ability to identify them by name.

The extra controllers can also operate accessory decoders, although the Select is limited to a maximum of 40 outputs (10 accessory decoders) compared to the Elite's 255 outputs.

Hornby also allow control of a moving locomotive to be passed from one controller to another without having to stop. This could be of benefit if you have an extra controller at a station or fiddle yard some distance from the main controller, or wish to follow your train around the layout.

The way that this works is that you select a locomotive as normal and set it running on a controller. On the second controller you enter the same locomotive's address. Moving the knob on EITHER controller will change the locomotive's speed. The display on the controller that is NOT currently operating the locomotive will flash to show that another controller is operating it.

This handover facility does mean that it is possible to accidentally take control of another operator's train if you enter the wrong locomotive address – one of the perils of multiple controller operation.

Any of the controllers can still be used for programming, but as the Select does not differentiate between a programming track and the main line, unlike the Elite, it is best not to use the Selects for this purpose.

To use a Select on the workbench simply unplug it from the XpressNet cable, and connect it to the power supply and track. Never plug two controllers on the same XpressNet into the mains as they will fight for control and may be damaged.

Despite the name the Select Walkabout offers only a limited ability to roam around the layout as it must be connected to the XpressNet by a cable at all times. If you disconnect the controller to move to a different location then it will need to power up when reconnected and will not remember which locomotive it was controlling.

When using the Hornby Select as a slave controller it is very important not to connect it to either a power supply or the track, only the XpressNet.

The Select controller is showing 'HC' on its display indicating that it has just powered up as a remote controller. The station operator can now shunt with the Class 25 in the foreground whilst the operator at the main controller can drive the DMU down the branch to the junction.

CHAPTER # Locomotive Decoders

Decoders come in a wide variety of shapes, sizes and with an array of features. All of these have a bearing on their suitability for use in a specific locomotive. Fortunately you can use any suitable decoder regardless of which type of command station you have. You may not be able to use all the command station features, or all the decoder features, but the basics will be compatible across the products of all suppliers.

As an example, if you have a command station that can only operate five functions you can still fit decoders with nine functions to your locomotives – it is just that four of the functions will never be used unless you upgrade the command station. Similarly if the command station can control more functions than the decoder then the extra functions will be ignored. The basics of speed, direction and address will be controllable regardless of how well matched the decoder and command station specifications are.

Before you even think about what type of decoder to fit in a locomotive you should ensure that it performs well on a standard DC power pack. DCC is not a magic cure for a bad motor or mechanism that is clogged with fluff. You will need to remove the model's body anyway so for models that have already clocked up a few miles it is a good opportunity to give the mechanism a good clean and to lubricate the gear trains. For a brand new model it is imperative to test it on DC so that you are happy with it before you start doing anything that might invalidate the guarantee.

Before You Start

One of the big problems faced by people who wish to convert locomotives to DCC operation is which decoder should they fit. There are a wide range of locomotive decoders available from a number of manufacturers. How can you possibly choose the right one for your needs?

The answer is to eliminate the decoders that aren't suitable and then pick from those that remain. Some people standardise on a particular decoder and only fit a different one if their chosen model just won't work in a given locomotive.

So what are the factors to consider when choosing a locomotive decoder?

Connection

Some models are now supplied 'DCC Ready' and come with a standard socket that a decoder can be plugged into. If you have such a model then you need a decoder with a plug. Other models need one which ends in wires. You can, of course, always convert a plug fitted decoder to a wire connection one by cutting the plug off – but as you will probably have paid extra for it in the first place you won't want to make a habit of it.

The Bachmann web site (www.bachmann.co.uk) includes a listing of the locomotives currently in their range that are fitted with a DCC socket. The socket blanking plug is also illustrated on the exploded diagram included with each locomotive, so you don't need to take the body off to establish if a socket is fitted.

Locomotive decoders come in a wide variety of sizes.

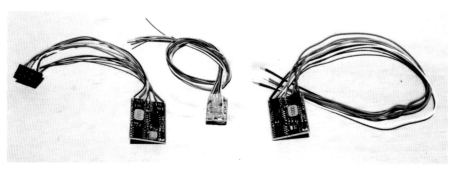

All Heljan locomotives are fitted with a DCC socket. For Hornby locomotives you can download service sheets from the Hornby web site (www.hornby.co.uk) which include an exploded diagram showing the DCC blanking plug, part number X9255, on locomotives fitted with a DCC socket.

Most decoders that have a plug fitted come with an NMRA eight-pin plug that matches the socket in most DCC ready locomotives. Large scale models, and the corresponding decoders, come with a 4-pin version designed for carrying higher currents whilst there is also a rarer 6-pin version intended for 'N' scale.

Some manufacturers mark pin number 1 on the socket, usually with a small triangle. If you can't work out which is pin 1 – don't worry, the connections have been specified so that it will not harm the locomotive or decoder if you plug it in the wrong way round. If you do plug the decoder in incorrectly, the locomotive may run but the lights won't work. Just unplug the decoder and plug it in the other way around.

Standard DCC plug/socket wiring (2 rows of 4 pins)

Pin	Wire Colour	Function
1	Orange	Motor +ve
2	Yellow	Rear Light (F0)
3	Green	F1
4	Black	Track pick up (left rail)
5	Grey	Motor –ve
6	White	Front light (F0)
7	Blue	Light/function common
8	Red	Track pick up (right rail)

Large scale DCC plug/socket wiring (2 rows of 2 pins)

Pin	Wire Colour	Function
1	Grey	Motor –ve
2	Orange	Motor +ve
3	Black	Track pick up (left rail)
4	Red	Track pick up (right rail)

Small DCC plug/socket wiring (1 row of 6 pins)

Pin	Wire Colour	Function
1	Orange	Motor +ve
2	Grey	Motor –ve
3	Red	Track pick up (right rail)
4	Black	Track pick up (left rail)
5	White	Front light (F0)
6	Yellow	Rear Light (F0)

The difference between conventional analogue (DC) wiring (below) and DCC wiring (bottom) inside a locomotive.

If you are installing a DCC decoder with wires rather than a plug then the diagram right shows how the decoder is connected between the track pick ups and the motor. The red decoder wire goes to the right rail (looking forwards) and the black one to the left rail. The orange wire goes to the motor terminal that was connected to the right rail, and the grey wire to the other motor terminal. If you get the red and black swapped around, or the grey and orange, all that will happen is that the locomotive will go backwards instead of forwards. However you must be careful not to mix up red and orange or grey and black as this will damage your decoder.

As DCC has developed the standard 8-pin plug used on many decoders has become a problem. The 8-pin layout allows for two wires to the track, two to the motor,

Analogue (DC) Locomotive Wiring

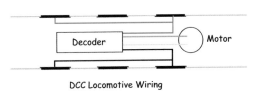

DCC Locomotive Wiring

a function common and three function wires (F0 forwards, F0 reverse and F1). With the coming of four-function decoders an extra wire was needed that has to be connected separately, similarly with sound decoders there are two extra wires for the loudspeaker. Clearly there is little point having a plug and socket for 8 wires when you have to solder or unsolder a further 3 wires when you install or remove a decoder, so something needed to happen.

The various standards for DCC are controlled by the National Model Railroad Association (NMRA), the national model railway society in the USA. They have a long consultation and committee process to agree any changes or extensions to the standards and the question of more decoder connections had been being discussed for a while. In the end Bachmann, and its associated brands, forced the issue in 2006 by adopting a proposed solution that had not yet been finally approved by the NMRA.

Whilst the new connectors, known as a 21-pin, seem to provide the potential for a large number of outputs, in fact they only cater for a maximum of five functions - the extra connections are for various odd and esoteric connections not commonly used - such is the problem with universal standards. The plugs and sockets are built into the locomotive and decoder circuit boards and the decoder is held in place by its socket - there are no wires to find space for and no special tricks are needed to fix the decoder in place.

Initially it was difficult to obtain suitable decoders for the limited number of 21-pin fitted locomotives produced for UK modellers. Fortunately many DCC producers have managed to introduce suitable items into their ranges so there is now a variety of decoders with different prices and facilities.

You can also purchase special 21- to 8-pin converters which allow you to plug an 8-pin decoder into a 21-pin fitted locomotive. The problem of mixing 21 and 8 pin fitted items is one of space. The converter takes up some of the space allocated for the 21-pin decoder and it can often be impossible to fit an 8-pin decoder and get the locomotive's body back on. One useful tip is to plug the 8-pin decoder into its socket before you push the converter onto the 21-pin plug – this avoids any risk of bending pins or damaging the converter.

Another difficulty that people have experienced with 21-pin decoders is that as there are no wires it is difficult to access a function output, either to re-route it or install an extra accessory. The 21-pin connector has the following connections, not that pin 11 is usually not present and acts as the marker so that the decoder is put on the right way around. The 8-pin connection was designed so that if it was plugged in the wrong way around the motor and pick-ups would still connect - just the functions wouldn't work. With the 21-pin design if you manage to get it in the wrong way round nothing will work. If you wish to use an extra function, for example to operate a smoke unit, then you need to find a suitable point to connect to the function output on the locomotive's circuit board.

21-pin plug/socket layout

22	21	20	19	18	17	16	15	14	13	12
1	2	3	4	5	6	7	8	9	10	11

21-pin Decoder Connections (8-pin equivalents in brackets)

1		8	F0 Forward (White/6)	15	F1 (Green)
2		9	Loudspeaker A	16	Function Common (Blue/7)
3		10	Loudspeaker B	17	
		11	Index - pin not present/	18	Motor -ve (Grey/5)
4	F4		socket blanked	19	Motor +ve (Orange/1)
5		12		20	
6		13	F3	21	Left rail power (Black/4)
7	F0 Reverse (Yellow/2)	14	F2 (Violet)	22	Right rail power (Red/8)

You need to be fairly gentle when removing the blanking plate and installing the new decoder. I have heard of people managing to pull some of the pins off the locomotive's circuit board when removing the blanking plate or bending them when pushing the decoder on.

One last thing, if you buy a Bachmann-DCC fitted locomotive with a 21-pin decoder fited the complicated looking green board in the box is not a spare decoder - it is the blanking plate to use if you ever wish to remove the decoder from the locomotive.

Key Facts:

Can I use a 21-pin decoder in a locomotive fitted with an 8-pin socket?
No, only in a locomotive with a 21-pin connection

Can I use a 21-pin decoder in a locomotive that is not DCC ready?
No. There is no way to connect wires to the decoder. Use a standard decoder with wires.

Can I use an 8-pin decoder in a locomotive fitted with a 21-pin connector?
You can buy a special converter, but it can be difficult to fit both the converter and 8-pin decoder in the space available.

Can I use a 21-pin decoder to run an extra accessory?
There are no wires that you can connect to accessories like smoke units. You need to find a connection on the locomotive's circuit board and use that.

The 21-pin connection has the plug on the locomotive's circuit board. You need to take care not to bend the pins when you remove the blanking plug or install the decoder.

The 21-pin decoder has a socket on its circuit board and no stray wires. The pins of the plug on the locomotive pass right through the socket on the decoder. From left to right there is a DC blanking plug, Bachmann decoder and a 21-pin to 8-pin converter.

The 21-pin to 8-pin converter allows a standard 8-pin decoder to be used with a 21-pin fitted locomotive. The problem is finding space for the converter, wire and decoder.

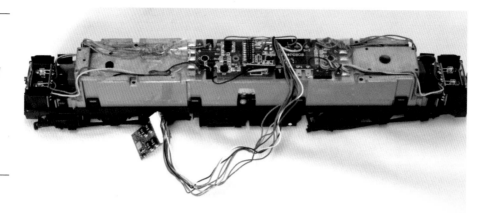

21-pin decoders do give a neat installation as there are no trailing wires and the locomotive has space for them designed in. This is a Bachmann decoder in place in a Bachmann Class 47 diesel locomotive.

This is what the wiring looks like on the locomotive side of a 21-pin DCC socket.

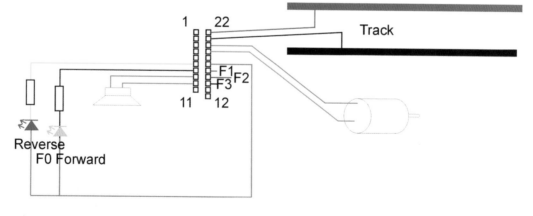

Size

Obvious really, but if it is too big to fit into whatever hidey hole is available in the locomotive then it just won't do. Some 8-pin and all 6 and 21-pin decoders have their plugs built into the circuit board so they just sit above the DCC socket. Other decoders have separate plugs with connecting wires and must be located somewhere within the model.

Check the dimensions of the decoder that you intend to use, and if you don't have one make a mock-up from cardboard, then see if it will fit. Don't forget that you will need space for the wires as well.

In some models finding space can be a big problem and it may be necessary to cut away parts of weights or the chassis. Don't forget useful hidey holes such as the fuel tanks underneath diesel locomotives and steam engine cabs and tenders.

Power Rating

Can the decoder provide enough power for the motor and anything else that it will be called on to operate, such as lights and smoke units? In general most Z or N gauge models draw 0.75A or less. Modern OO or HO models typically draw less than 1A, with older ones needing up to 1.5A. O gauge and larger models can draw as much as 4A. If you fit a decoder intended for an N gauge model in your O gauge class 47 it will have a pretty short lifespan.

You will often read that it is necessary to know, or determine, the stall current of a locomotive before you fit a decoder. To establish the stall current you will need to connect a meter between a conventional DC power pack and the track and set it to a suitable Amp scale then hold the locomotive so that the wheels cannot rotate and give it a burst of full power. This is a fairly risky process as you may damage the model or its motor. In truth there is no need to precisely measure the stall current as decoders come with a limited range of current capacities. For an electric locomotive to be drawing the stall current it would need to either have something wedged in the gears or wheels in order to bring it to a complete halt. Even the worst derailment will normally leave the wheels free to rotate so a complete stop is a fairly unlikely eventuality. It is far more important that your chosen decoder can provide the current needed for normal continuous running. By and large models built in the past few years have a lower current consumption than those built years ago.

Addresses

Some decoders only support locomotive addresses up to 99 (called 2-digit addressing) whilst others go up to 9999 (4-digit addressing). If your DCC system only supports 2-digit addressing then you can buy either type. If you never intend to use more than 99 locomotives, or use your locomotives on another layout which might, then you can use 2-digit decoders. If your DCC system offers 4-digit addressing then it is probably better to only use 4-digit decoders.

Functions

How many accessories do you want to operate? For most UK outline models this is usually limited to lights and one function (F0) will cope with normal directional lighting.

The function outputs can do all sorts of things – provided that the model is equipped to use them. Lighting is a favourite feature and to correctly replicate modern UK practice you need four function outputs. Other features that are suitable for function control include horns or whistles, remote control uncoupling and smoke generators.

Whilst some new locomotives produced for the UK market now include factory fitted lights, many still do not. If you wish to install lighting Express Models supply kits for many diesel classes and oil type head and tail lamps for steam outline models.

Motor Control

More expensive decoders tend to offer facilities to improve the control of the locomotive's motor similar to DC feedback controllers, offer shunting modes and high frequency operation for high quality coreless motors.

Sound

The range of sounds available for UK models is increasing slowly. Whilst sound equipped decoders are expensive they are very impressive, especially as the sound is automatically matched to the motion of the model.

One problem with sound-equipped decoders is finding room for the larger sized decoder and accompanying speaker. In 4mm scale diesel locomotives the between bogies fuel tank is one possible place for hiding the speaker. As technology advances these units are becoming smaller and it is now possible to obtain decoders and speakers to fit into 'N' scale locomotives. Another problem is that the range of UK locomotive sounds available is limited at the moment but it is expanding all the time.

When installing a sound-equipped decoder you should always try to fit the largest speaker that the locomotive can accommodate as this will give better sound quality and volume. In addition rectangular speakers, where available, usually have a better frequency response and are preferable to circular ones.

Never fit a sound system to a noisy locomotive as the mechanical noise will drown out that expensive sound. Similarly you should not fit sound systems to locomotives fitted with old open frame motors as these can often generate radio frequency interference which may be picked up by the decoder circuitry. If possible you should always try to use locomotives fitted with high-quality 'can' motors for this type of installation.

If you have a small layout then you could opt to install the sound-equipped decoder underneath the layout, rather than in a locomotive. It would need to be wired into the track bus and could be used in conjunction with any suitable locomotive. To operate it you would simply use the DCC consist facility that enables a number of locomotives to be operated as a set. This would mean that the decoder's sounds would reflect the locomotive's operation. Mounting the decoder under the layout would also allow the use of a much larger speaker with an improvement in sound quality. You could, of course, install a number of decoders in this way so that you could have a number of different locomotives apparently producing sound at the same time and match the type of sound to the type of locomotive.

Sound-equipped decoders for UK outline models are available from a number of suppliers, mainly using ESU LokSound decoders. In addition Bachmann and Hornby market ready-to-run locomotives equipped with DCC decoders and sound.

One last warning; sound-equipped decoders are very easily damaged so make sure that you read, and follow, the instructions supplied with them.

Special Features and Extra Functions

Some decoders have special features such as automatic braking, auxiliary power supplies and bi-directional communications. If you want to use facilities such as these then you will probably be very restricted in your choice of decoder. In addition some decoder ranges have special features that match their manufacturer's command stations. If you wish to use these features then you are tied to specific decoders.

One of the things that many newcomers to DCC find mystifying is the wide variation in prices for locomotive decoders. This difference is largely due to the features that are included. Some decoders only support a limited number of configuration variables (CVs) which limits their flexibility. Others may have extra power, a smaller size or more function outputs. Many of the more expensive decoders have sophisticated systems for getting the best performance out of your locomotives including feedback (back-EMF monitoring) and other techniques for different types of motor.

People keep on finding extra uses for the function outputs of decoders. Express Models supply lighting kits for modern diesel locomotives that use eight functions just for the lights. These are: (1) Forward marker lights. (2) Reverse marker lights (3) Forward tail lights (4) Reverse tail lights. (5) Forward white headlight (6) Reverse white headlight (7) Forward cab interior light. (8) Reverse cab interior light. Add sound, operating fans, remote uncoupling, a smoke unit and you have a lot of functions.

If you need more functions than are available on a standard decoder then it is possible to install a second 'function only' decoder, such as the Lenz LX100F in the locomotive. This type of decoder has function outputs but no motor control circuitry. You can install several function-only decoders in the same locomotive to work in combination with the locomotive decoder or install a function-only decoder by itself in a piece of rolling stock that does not need motor control, such as the trailing power car in a multiple unit set.

If you install multiple decoders in the same locomotive, you will have to make sure that you can program the decoders independently and you might have to carry out the programming before installation. If you are using decoders in different vehicles of a set, such as a multiple unit, then each decoder can be programmed individually by placing each vehicle on the programming track in turn. In both cases all the decoders should be set to the same locomotive address.

Support and Availability

Good support, such as a 'no questions asked' replacement policy, or ready availability from the shelves of your local model shop may also be important to you.

Where should you buy DCC decoders from? Anywhere that can offer you the item you need, at a price you can afford and with service that you are happy with. This can be a mail order or internet retailer, model shop or eBay auction – whichever you feel happy with.

Installation

Many guides to decoder installation suggest that you should remove the suppression devices, such as chokes and capacitors, from locomotives as part of the process. These components are there to stop the models generating electro-magnetic radiation that can interfere with electrical and electronic items ranging from televisions and computers through to police radios and pacemakers. These components have been installed in order that the locomotive will comply with current EU legislation.

Chokes should always be left in place as they do not affect the operation of the decoder. With some installations the capacitors can cause poor or erratic running. Some modern examples contain RF suppression components in the decoder and so the locomotive's capacitors can be removed. Others do not and in such cases the locomotive's capacitors should be retained. You should refer to the decoder manufacturer's instructions to find out the specific recommendation for each decoder. The best approach appears to be to leave the capacitors in place and only remove them if the locomotive's performance under DCC is poor or erratic when compared to its performance prior to conversion.

Before you begin any installation work you should ensure that the locomotive that you are converting to DCC operates well under conventional DC. Putting a decoder in will not cure a bad motor, binding gears or bent valve gear. Old locomotives should be cleaned and serviced before conversion. Ideally new locomotives should be run in – remember in many cases installing a DCC decoder will involve you in work that will invalidate the manufacturer's warranty, so make sure that the locomotive is not faulty in any way before you start.

It is a good idea to keep a record of what type of decoder you have fitted in each locomotive and what your CV settings are. This will enable you to reset the CV settings if they get changed by accident.

Whilst some locomotives can be converted to DCC easily, others can be challenging. An increasing number of model shops and individuals are offering DCC conversion services and if you are nervous about converting a particular model then you may wish to use such a service. Whilst this does push the cost of the conversion up it does guarantee that you will get a working DCC locomotive.

Whilst it is imperative that decoders are insulated from the chassis, pick-ups and motor it is not advisable to cover them with heatshrink tubing or insulating tape. Many decoders generate heat and if it cannot escape into the air they may overheat and cease to work. Some manufacturers supply decoders wrapped in a plastic coating, these are fine and have been designed that way but if your chosen decoder is not wrapped, leave it like that.

Tools of the Trade

You will need a small selection of tools and materials to install decoders in your locomotives.

- Electrical meter which can give a resistance (Ohm) reading. These will normally also offer other measurements, typically AC and DC voltage (Volts) and current (Amps).

    A simple one priced at around ten pounds or less is perfectly adequate for the job and is invaluable for solving electrical problems on any model railway.
- Wire strippers. Using proper wire strippers is far superior to attempting to strip the insulation with a knife. The strippers ensure that the insulation is removed cleanly and leave all the wire strands intact. There is also no danger of the knife slipping and cutting your finger.
- Small screwdrivers. For removing locomotive bodies and other assorted parts.
- Soldering Iron. An electrical soldering iron with a small bit is needed for making electrical connections. If you also need to solder whitemetal kits you should use a different bit (or even a different iron) as electrical and whitemetal solders do not mix well.
- Soldering Iron Stand. You should have somewhere safe to put your soldering iron when you are not actually using it to make a connection. A purpose designed stand means that there is less chance of a hot soldering iron escaping. As an aside, never try to catch a falling soldering iron. The power cable will tend to make it fall with the hot bit uppermost which is where you will be most likely to grab it, leading to badly burnt fingers. The alternative tactic of trying to catch the lead will cause the iron to swing in an arc and burn you somewhere else. Let it drop and then retrieve it quickly.
- Solder. Electrical solder has the flux incorporated in it.
- Heat Shrink Tubing. Used to cover bare wires and stop accidental short circuits. Can be obtained from electronics suppliers such as Maplin Electronics and Rapid Electronics.

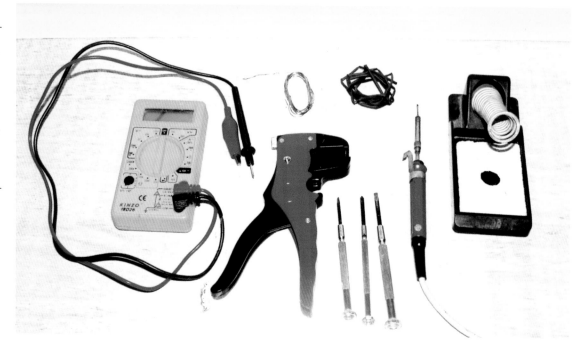

The tools needed to install DCC decoders in your locomotives. Clockwise from the left: electrical meter, solder, heat shrink tubing, soldering iron stand, soldering iron, small screwdrivers and wire strippers.

Joining two wires

To make a good electrical and mechanical connection between two wires is a simple process. First you strip about a centimetre of insulation from each of the wires to be joined.

Cut a length of heat shrink tubing a little longer than the longest of the bare sections of wire and thread it on to one of the lengths of wire. Now twist the two bare wires together.

Put the hot soldering iron on the twisted wires and let them heat up. With the soldering iron still in place touch the end of the solder to the twisted wires (not the soldering iron). The solder will melt and flow around the wires. Remove the solder and the iron and allow the joint to cool.

Bend the soldered joint so that it runs parallel to one of the wires. Slide the heat shrink tubing along until it completely covers the soldered joint. Now hold your soldering iron alongside the tubing which will shrink and encase the soldered joint.

You now have a connection that will conduct electricity, resist being pulled apart and not be susceptible to short circuits if it comes into contact with other connections.

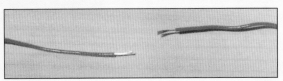

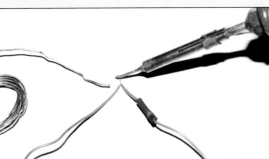

Hornby Class 31 Diesel

The Hornby Class 31 is advertised as being 'DCC ready'. In simple terms this means that it is fitted with an 8-pin socket so that a decoder can be plugged in. Actually doing it, however, is not quite so easy.

First of all you need to check that the locomotive works correctly on conventional DC, either using a DC controller or by running it as an analogue locomotive (usually number 0) on your DCC controller.

Once you are happy with its performance you can start to dismantle the locomotive. If you turn it upside down you will see four screws, one either side of the bogies. These are large standard screws. Don't unscrew the small crosshead screws in front of the bogies – these are for the buffer beam fairings. The large screws are hard to get out so you may find it easier to leave them in their holes.

You will need a small flat bladed screwdriver to release the body. There are four screws, one on each side of the two bogies.

At first glace there doesn't appear to be anywhere obvious to fit the decoder. In fact there is a compartment under the circuit board seen on the left.

You will need a small crosshead screwdriver to unscrew the circuit board. There are two screws, diagonally opposite each other.

Be careful when you lift the circuit board otherwise you may disconnect some of the wires. The decoder compartment is small and enclosed.

The decoder's wires need to come up through an opening in the circuit board and then plug into the socket. Make sure that pin 1 on the plug aligns with pin 1 marked on the socket.

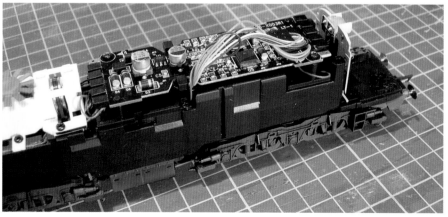

The cab interiors have tail lights mounted on them which plug into contacts on the chassis. If they come away from the body you can have difficulty getting the lights to work again. If you do experience problems stick them to the chassis with double-sided adhesive tape.

It's getting dark, so on with the lights. All finished and ready to roll.

Turn the model the right way up and the body should just slide up and come away from the chassis. If you have left the screws in place, push them up and hold them there with a little Blu-tack.

Lever the blanking plug out of the socket on the circuit board and put that somewhere safe in case you ever wish to refit it. The decoder location is situated underneath the circuit board in the locomotive, so this needs to be unscrewed as well. It is held in place by two small crosshead screws at either corner of the board. Keep these in a safe place.

Gently lift the circuit board and you will see that there is not much space available so you will need to use a small decoder. Suitable candidates include the Lenz Gold and TCS M1. Hornby supply a sleeve to put over the decoder to insulate it from the chassis. Do not use it. Decoders that come without a wrapper are designed to be left unwrapped to dissipate the heat that they produce. Wrapping them can cause the decoder to fail. Decoders that come with a wrapper already on are designed to work that way and so are a better choice in this situation.

Attach the decoder to the underside of the circuit board with a sticky pad and then route the wires as shown in the photo. Screw the circuit board in place and plug the cable into the socket, making sure that pin 1 (the orange wire) on the plug aligns with pin 1 as marked on the circuit board. You can now test the installation on your programming track.

The cab interiors are lightly glued into the body and are supposed to clip onto contacts on the chassis so that the lights get power. This is a weak point in the design and one of my cabs came loose. I spent quite a while trying to get both cabs to sit correctly before giving up and fixing the errant cab interior to the chassis with a small strip of double-sided adhesive tape. This meant a bit more jiggling to get the body back on, but ensured that I had working lights at both ends.

Now screw the four screws in the chassis back up and check that everything is still working. Congratulations, you have successfully finished the installation.

Hornby Britannia

When people think of difficult locomotives to convert to DCC the first that spring to mind always seem to be small shunters. Whilst this is understandable it may come as a surprise to the uninitiated that large tender steam locomotives can be equally challenging. The reason for this is simple, in order to get the type of performance that we have come to expect from the current generation of models it is necessary to pack every available space with weight in order to maximise both haulage and electrical pick-up. The practical upshot of this is that despite the overall bulk of a model like the Hornby Britannia class, there is precious little space inside to fit a decoder.

The current Hornby Britannia has been released in two different versions, one with a tender drive and the other with the motor mounted in the locomotive itself. A quick guide to which is shown below so that if you are considering buying one, you can establish which variant it is.

Number	Name	Hornby Ref.	Drive
70000	Britannia	R2562	Locomotive
70013	Oliver Cromwell	R2565	Locomotive
70015	Apollo	R2717/R2717X	Locomotive
70018	Flying Dutchman	R2387	Tender
70030	William Wordsworth	R2563	Locomotive
70036	Boadicea	R2484	Tender
70037	Hereward the Wake	R2619	Locomotive
70038	Robin Hood	R2719/R2719X	Locomotive
70046	Anzac	R2457	Tender
70050	Firth of Clyde	R2718/R2718X	Locomotive
70052	Firth of Tay	R2564	Locomotive

Always test a new locomotive on conventional DC before converting it to DCC operation. If there are any problems with it, it is easier to get them sorted out now before you start to take it apart. Here Boadicea is being run from a DC controller. You can also perform the DC test by using address 0 on some DCC controllers.

The tender-drive versions are the easiest to convert to DCC, especially given the new generation of decoders that have no leads and just plug directly into the DCC 8-pin socket provided in many DCC ready locomotives.

The first step in any DCC conversion is to test the locomotive on conventional DC, either by using a DC controller or running it as an analogue locomotive (address 0) on your DCC controller. Remember that fitting a DCC decoder will not cure a faulty locomotive.

The Tender Drive Version

On the tender drive version the DCC socket is situated in the tender. The tender body simply pulls off by applying pressure at both ends and then pulling the chassis down. It only takes a matter of seconds to separate the two parts. Remove the dummy plug from the DCC socket, replace with a Lenz Silver Direct and put the tender on the test track to test the installation. Once you have confirmed that everything is OK push the tender body back on and you are ready to go. It really is that simple.

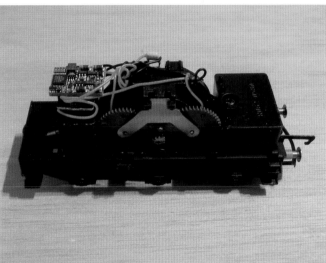

ABOVE LEFT: *The tender body simply pulls off once you press in the ends. The dummy plug in the DCC socket can be seen on the right. You may need to loosen the wires from the knot over the motor to make enough room to remove the dummy plug.*

ABOVE: *This is the Lenz Silver Direct in place in Boadicea's tender. The tender can be tested on its own without needing to be coupled to the locomotive. Both the locomotive and the tender are fitted with electrical pick-ups which improves the locomotive's performance.*

LEFT: *After a quick test under DCC control you can replace the tender body and the locomotive is ready to use.*

The top of the Hornby packaging makes a useful cradle to hold the locomotive whilst you are fitting a decoder.

The Locomotive Drive Version

Compared to the tender drive version the locomotive drive Britannia is far more awkward. Given the high level of fine detail some form of cradle to hold the model whilst you are working on it is a must. Fortunately the top section of the model's packaging fits the bill. To fit a decoder you will need small crosshead and flat-bladed screwdrivers and a pair of pliers or set of small spanners. If you intend to use the Lenz Silver Direct decoder you will also need a pair of side-cutters and a craft knife.

The first step is to use the pliers or small spanners to undo the bolt that secures the speedo cable to the left-hand side coupling rod. Once the cable has been disconnected replace the bolt to stop it getting lost. If you try to remove the chassis without disconnecting the cable you will damage the cable or its fixings.

Before you can get at the body mounting screw you need to remove the pony truck. This is secured by two small crosshead screws. Once you have taken these out put them in the decoder box to keep them safe. You can now slide the pony truck forwards and lift it out. You should now see two screws, one large and one small. Do not undo the small crosshead screw. To release the body you need to undo the large screw with a flat-bladed screwdriver. Once the large screw has been removed you can pull the front of the chassis down and then forwards to separate it from the body. When you do this the two lubricators will come away from the footplate and dangle loosely. Don't worry – this is supposed to happen.

The decoder socket is in the middle of the chassis. Remove the dummy plug and install the decoder. There is no need to remove the capacitor as the Lenz decoder functions happily with it left in place. Use some adhesive tape or Blu-tack to hold the lubricators in place whilst you test the decoder installation.

There are two ribs on the inside of the boiler that need to be removed if you are fitting the Lenz decoder. Use a pair of side cutters to trim them down and cut off any remaining waste with a craft knife.

Reuniting the body and chassis is a trying task. It requires a fair amount of force to get the rear locating lug to fit into place. You need about four hands to keep the two lubricators, speedo cable and tender wires under control as you ease the chassis in. The lubricators need to be fitted between the footplate and chassis before the chassis is pushed fully home. Once the chassis has been screwed back in you can reconnect the speedo cable and attach the pony truck. Couple up the tender, plug in the wires and you are ready to roll.

RIGHT: *You need to remove the bolt that connects the speedo cable to the connecting rod otherwise you will break the cable when you remove the chassis. If you don't have a set of small spanners then fine-nosed pliers will do the job.*

CENTRE LEFT: *Using a small crosshead screwdriver you need to undo the two screws that hold the pony truck in place so that you can gain access to the body retaining screw.*

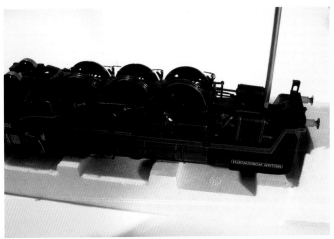

ABOVE: *Once the pony truck has been removed you can unscrew the large retaining screw with a flat-bladed screwdriver.*

LEFT: *By pulling down then forwards the chassis will now slide out from the body.*

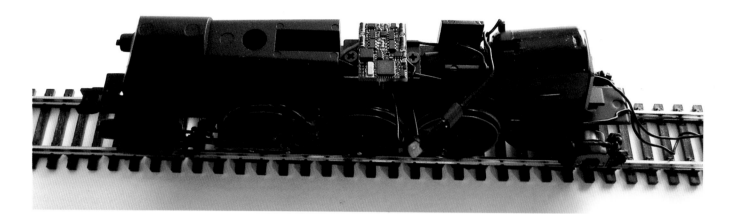

ABOVE: The Lenz decoder in place on the chassis. The brown bead with wires attached is a capacitor to reduce TV interference when run on DC.

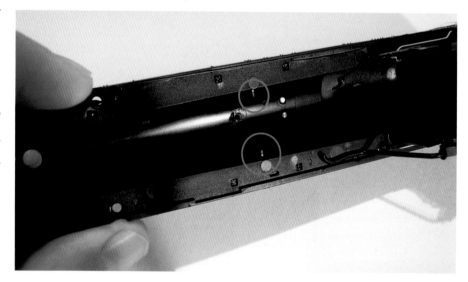

CENTRE: There are two ribs inside the boiler that will need to be cut away if you intend to fit the Lenz Silver Direct decoder.

RIGHT: The ribs can be cut away using a pair of side cutters.

Putting the model back together is an interesting task. The lubricators, circled, need to be guided back into position as you push the chassis home.

Bachmann Ivatt 2-6-2T

There are some models that are best described as 'challenging' when it comes to fitting a DCC decoder. Amongst these are some of the older Bachmann models that have a split chassis. These models have a chassis that is divided into two electrically live halves separated by insulating spacers. In theory there is no difference in fitting a DCC decoder to a split-chassis locomotive than any other, but in practice it involves virtually complete dis-assembly of the model.

This installation is on an Ivatt 2-6-2T, but the same procedure is needed for Bachmann's A4, B1, V2, V1/3, J72, J39, Lord Nelson, Manor, 43xx/53xx/93xx/47xx, Hall, original Jubilee, Scot and Patriot 4MT and 04 diesel shunter. The split-chassis locomotives tend to be short on space within the body so most decoder fitting services actually remove some of the chassis block to make room. On this installation I have chosen to use a small decoder placed in the loco's cab. This is invisible in normal use and is a lot easier than trying to remove bits of the chassis with a hacksaw.

From the outside you can't tell the difference, but this Bachmann Ivatt tank now has a DCC decoder installed.

The selected decoder is a TCS M3 – I would have used an M1 as I don't need the extra function outputs but with the vagaries of exchange rate movements and stock levels the M3 was actually cheaper. It is always worth comparing prices when you buy a decoder, it is surprising how much they can vary.

The TCS M1 and M3 are small decoders measuring about 0.6in (15.25mm) by 0.4in (10mm) and less than 0.2in (5mm) tall. There are various harness options, but we just need wires. If you get a good deal on one with a plug, simply cut the plug off. The TCS decoders come in a plastic coat so you don't have to worry about insulating the decoder from the loco. If you choose an alternative decoder that comes without a cover then be very careful with your insulation – if the decoder touches the chassis it will have a very short life expectancy.

The victim is placed in a foam cradle to prevent damage to the bodywork.

One of the problems with fitting DCC decoders is that it is very easy to damage the locomotive whilst you are doing it. A foam cradle will help keep the locomotive still and safe whilst you are tinkering with its chassis. The one illustrated is made by Peco and is available in most model shops.

Disassembly varies from model to model, but they all follow the same pattern. First remove the screws securing the body, remove that and put it somewhere safe. I use an old ice cream tub to keep all the bits in whilst work is in progress. This ensures that no vital parts get lost. Leading and trailing pony trucks or bogies are unscrewed next, watching out for any springs or washers that might make a bid for freedom. Remove any plastic brake rigging, if fitted and then unscrew the keeper plate from the bottom of the chassis.

The body and pony trucks have been removed and the chassis replaced in the cradle. By now you will be wishing that you had never started, but there are still more bits to come off. The brake rigging (top) was removed gently and then the keeper plate (left) was unscrewed and lifted off.

The next step is to disconnect the cylinders from the chassis. Gentle persuasion with a small screwdriver is usually needed.

To remove the wheels you will first of all need to pull the cylinders off the chassis. They come off sideways, not forwards, and you will almost certainly need to use a small screwdriver to help prise them off. Be gentle and take your time, the valve gear is delicate and easily damaged. If you cannot get them off then it is still possible to remove the wheels, but getting the valve gear back in place when you reassemble the model is much harder.

With the cylinders disconnected the valve gear is still connected to the chassis. You can either pull the plastic mounting off or undo the small screw that holds it in place.

The valve gear is held in place by a plastic moulding and small screw between the first and second axle. You have a choice here in that you can either prise the moulding off, making replacement easier, or undo the screw. Once you have done that you can lift the wheels out of the chassis block.

Taking the chassis block out of the cradle, you can lay it on its side and undo the screws that join the two halves. The two halves are separated by small plastic spacers; be very careful not to lose them when you separate them. You will probably have to resort to more gentle persuasion from a screwdriver to get the two parts to separate.

There are two springs which provide electrical connections to the motor. Don't worry if these spring out when you separate the chassis – they are the only bits that

With the valve gear disconnected from the chassis you can lift the wheels out. The coupling rods are left attached to the wheels.

The chassis block consists of two sides that are screwed together. Be careful not to lose any of the plastic spacers when you separate them.

At last! With the two halves of the chassis separated we can finally get at the motor.

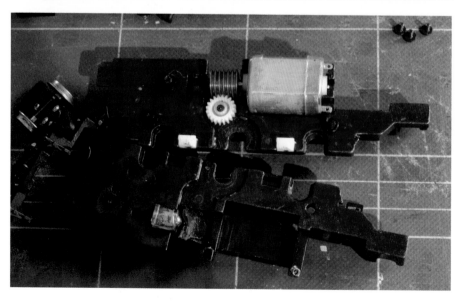

The orange decoder wire has been cut to length and connected to the motor ready for soldering. Don't forget to put a length of heat-shrink tubing on the wire before you connect it up.

you won't need to put back. Before you lift the motor out make a note of which way up it goes and which tag is connected to the right hand side of the chassis. This is usually marked with a red dot; if it isn't, it might be a good time to do so with a felt-tip pen.

The orange wire from the decoder will be connected to the terminal with the red dot; the grey one will go to the other terminal. To insulate them from the chassis you will need to use a length of heat-shrink tubing. Don't forget to slide this onto the wire before you connect it to the motor. The wires should be cut to length; this will vary depending on where you have decided to fit the decoder. Solder the wires in place, slide the heat-shrink tubing over so that it covers the whole tag and connection. It is vital that there is no bare wire, tag or solder as this will cause a short that will destroy your decoder.

Before you replace the motor check that you have removed the two small springs that connected it to the chassis and, while you are at it, remove any grot or fluff from the worm and gear.

Don't forget to remove the two springs that connected the motor to the chassis. They are the only parts that you should discard.

With the motor back in place we can start to put everything together again.

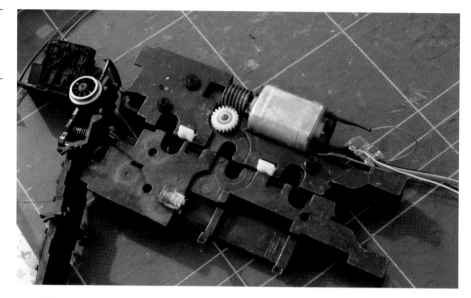

With the motor in place you can start to rebuild the locomotive. Check that the motor is the same way up as it was when you started and that the worm and gear mesh nicely. You can now put the two halves of the chassis together and replace the screws.

The next step is the trickiest part of the whole exercise, getting the wheels back in and the valve gear in place. If you have a digital camera then you might find it worthwhile to take a picture of both sides of the locomotive before you start – there are a surprising number of rods and they all need to be in the right alignment if you want the locomotive to run when you have finished. Once everything is back in place put the cylinders on and reattach the keeper plate and pony trucks.

The decoder's black wire needs to be soldered to the copper tag on the left hand side of the chassis whilst the red wire is attached to the tag on the right hand side.

On the Ivatt there are two copper plates attached to the chassis; these are ideal locations to solder the red and black decoder wires. The red wire goes on the right hand side of the chassis, looking forwards, and the black wire to the left. Now is the time for a test run before the body goes back on.

You can cut the function wires off if you don't want to install lighting. If you wish to keep your options open then trim them back a bit to make them easier to conceal. I cut a little of the plastic cab interior moulding away so that it was easier to get the wires in place. Stick the decoder to the cab floor with a bit of double-sided tape. A small bit of adhesive tape over the top will hold the wires in place, with a dollop of black paint to conceal everything from view. Now put the body back on and you're ready to go.

With the cab interior back in place and the decoder stuck down we are nearly finished.

A bit of adhesive tape will hold the wires in place, with some black paint over the top to conceal everything from view.

Graham Farish Class 57 Diesel ('N' gauge)

So far this chapter has concentrated on DCC in general and 4 mm scale in particular. DCC is, of course, suitable for other scales and gauges but they all present their own particular problems and pitfalls. In this example I shall look at fitting a decoder to one of Graham Farish's diesels that is promoted as 'DCC Ready'.

'DCC Ready' can have a different meaning in this context than it does in 4mm scale. Instead of having a socket to plug a decoder into, there are positions on the model's circuit board to which the decoder wires can be soldered. This may come as a surprise but it is a great advance over the difficulties that can be experienced fitting decoders to older Graham Farish designs.

The victim, in this case, is a Class 57 diesel and, as usual, it needs to be tested on standard DC before you start messing around with the innards. If you are totally DCC and don't possess a DC controller then you can connect your intended decoder between the controller and your test track for testing and running in purposes.

Graham Farish supply some instructions covering DCC conversion with the model, but it is not uncommon to find that these have slipped out of the box. They can be downloaded from the Bachmann website, but are well hidden. You need to go to the Service page and download the Graham Farish GE Class 66 instructions (the Class 66 uses the same chassis). To go directly to the instructions, type this address into your web browser:
http://www. bachmann.co.uk/pdfs/ GF_66_Decoder.pdf.

The problem with N gauge models is that there is a distinct lack of space for a decoder, even in something as large as a Class 57.
To the right of the locomotive is the TCS M1 decoder that I used, to the left is a normal-sized decoder from ZTC.

There are four small clips, one in each corner, that hold the body in place. The body can be removed by running your fingernails along the gap between the body sides and the chassis; this gentle pressure will release the clips so that you can drop the chassis out.

Some releases of the Class 57 and the Class 60 have a design fault whereby the connection from the circuit board to the motor can short against the chassis block. Whilst this can cause mysterious short circuits under DC operation, under DCC such a short will destroy the locomotive's decoder so it is imperative to sort this problem out before continuing with the installation.

RIGHT: Once you have got the body off, this is the sight that greets you. At either end there are small circuit boards for the lighting that slip into guides in the chassis block. They are connected by wires to the main circuit board which is held in position by two cross-head screws. The decoder connections are underneath the two metal tabs on the lower right-hand side of the circuit board.

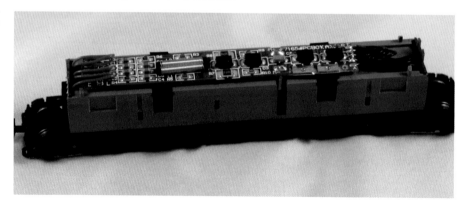

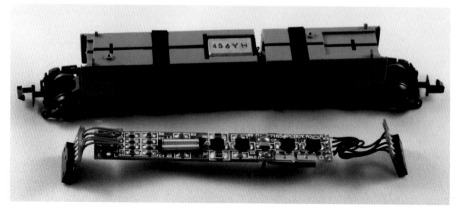

LEFT: With the circuit board removed you can see the problem area. The two copper arms that come down underneath the circuit board can touch the chassis block and short circuit the model. Annoying with DC, this will destroy a DCC decoder.

To remove the circuit board you need to unscrew the two small cross-head screws at opposite corners of the board using a small jeweller's screwdriver. Put them somewhere safe and then slide the two lighting boards out of their guides at each end of the chassis. Now lift the main circuit board out and put it to one side.

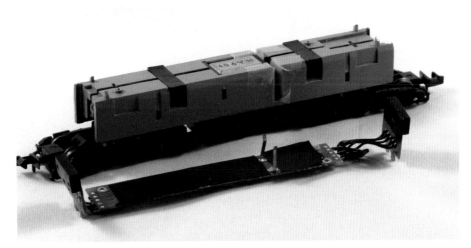

Fixing the potential short is a few minutes' work with some parcel tape. The black tape underneath the circuit board is factory fitted to stop the board shorting on the chassis block.

To insulate the chassis block I used brown parcel tape (the self-adhesive variety, not the sort that you need to lick). This is thin, flexible and has strong adhesive. I cut a small piece, pushed it in place with a cocktail stick, folded it back along the chassis side, cut the free section of tape down the fold and then pushed the two tabs down onto the top of the chassis. I did this for all four faces of the central well, being careful to keep the drive shaft and motor tags free of tape.

Once the tape was in place I reinstalled the circuit board, but not the body, and checked that the model still worked on DC, just to be sure that I hadn't impeded the drive train or disrupted the electrical contacts. After that, it was off with the circuit board again and this time the chassis was put to one side.

As an N scale locomotive is half as long as its 4mm scale equivalent there is only one-eighth of the volume available inside, thus most N gauge models need small decoders. I chose a TCS M1, supplied by Bromsgrove Models, which comes wrapped in an insulating sleeve which makes installation just a little bit easier. The seven wires from the decoder need to be trimmed to length and then stripped ready for soldering to the circuit board. I decided to mount the decoder next to the circuit board connections so some of the wires ended up quite short. My preference is to cut each wire to length in turn as this gives less scope for error. I also left a little excess on each wire to give some flexibility when positioning the decoder.

The decoder connections are hidden under two metal tags that route the DC supply. These should be removed by gently levering them off using a small screwdriver. With the decoder connections towards you on the top of the board the sequence for connecting the wires seems strange, but is arranged for simplicity of the DC connections.

Levering off the metal tags at the edge of the circuit board reveals the contacts where the decoder's wires will be soldered.

From left to right the sequence is:

8	Red	Right rail pick-up
1	Orange	Motor
2	Yellow	Lights - forward
4	Black	Left rail pick-up
5	Grey	Motor
6	White	Lights - reverse
7	Blue	Lights - common

If you have a decoder which supports functions over and above directional lighting then you will have extra wires that need to be trimmed back and insulated.

Each connection needs to be soldered in place, being careful not to bridge adjoining pads on the circuit board with either wire or solder. Work slowly, carefully and ideally check the connections on both sides of the board with a magnifier.

The decoder's wires are cut to length and soldered to the appropriate contact. Another bit of parcel tape on the chassis block will help to ensure that there are no unexpected shorts. Once the board is back in place a quick test should confirm that all is well.

Once you are happy with your handiwork add some insulation to the top of the chassis under the connections, parcel tape again, replace the circuit board and test the chassis under DCC. If all is well the model should respond to address 3 and the directional lighting will turn on and off when you press F0. If you get lights but the model will not move you need to check that the connections from the circuit board to the motor are actually pressing against the motor's tags and haven't got bent whilst you were working on it.

With everything working you can fix the decoder in place (yet more parcel tape), replace the body and you are ready to go.

The decoder is held in place with another length of parcel tape and then the body can be replaced. Job done!

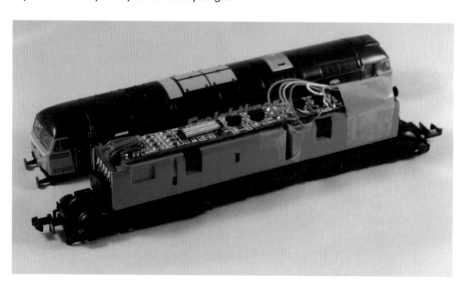

Hornby Class 25 Diesel

Whilst it is relatively easy to fit a DCC decoder to model locomotives that have been designed in the past few years many of us have older locomotives that were designed before DCC was invented. Converting these to DCC can vary from straightforward through to virtually impossible, depending on the particular model. In this section I shall look at one of the straightforward types, a Hornby diesel powered by a Ringfield motor bogie.

The Ringfield motor was used in many Hornby locomotives for many years and is still capable of giving good service. It can be found in both tender-drive steam locomotives and diesels such as my chosen victim, a Class 25. There were two basic types of Ringfield motor: one is an easy DCC conversion, the other requires a bit more work. This example is the 'easy' one; the harder one can be distinguished by screws at the top of the brush retaining arms – those large metal fingers on the side of the motor.

Before you start on a DCC conversion of a locomotive like this it is vital to check that it is in good running order. The first step is to clean the wheels and get any grot out from the pickups. If the decoder doesn't get a constant, reliable supply of electricity it isn't going to work well, if at all. Once you can get reliable medium speed running then you are okay to proceed – don't worry too much about slow speed performance; that should improve with a good decoder.

The body was unclipped and the rats' nest that powered the headcode lights was removed. The bogies were unclipped and the gears on the motor bogie checked and cleaned. To make it easy to strip the locomotive down for future maintenance I decided to use the original Hornby connectors for the lights, pick-ups and motor. So the wire from the unpowered bogie was removed, cut in half and the two cut ends stripped. The same fate befell the wire connecting the pick-ups on the motor bogie to the lighting circuit. A small black wire on the front of the motor bogie connecting the pick-ups to the motor was removed and discarded.

Take one elderly locomotive... This is a Hornby Class 25 diesel which is old enough to vote, drink and have a family. Whilst it is not worth a great deal in financial terms there are a lot of models like this that are worth more to their owners than can be realised by selling them on.

Inside the model there is an early directional lighting installation – in this case it illuminates the headcode. It is interesting to note that there is provision for fitting a smoke generator.

RIGHT: *Once the chassis has been dismantled we can strip much of the old wiring out. Hang on to the diodes though, they may come in useful one day.*

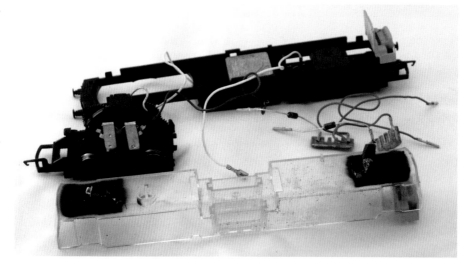

BELOW: *By re-using the Hornby wires it will be possible to disconnect the decoder from the motor and trailing bogies for routine maintenance. The wires can be joined by twisting them together, soldering and then covering with heat-shrink sleeving for insulation.*

ABOVE: *The Hornby Ringfield motor was used in many Hornby locomotives over the years. One thing to be aware of is that there were two patterns – one of which needs more work when you are converting it for DCC operation. This one is the easy version – the other one has screws in the top of the brush retaining arms.*

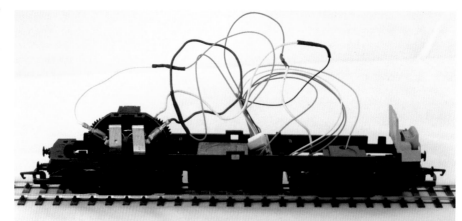

LEFT: *The first test of the decoder, looking more like a bird's nest than a locomotive. This is to check that the locomotive works, goes the right way and to see if the capacitor needs to be removed.*

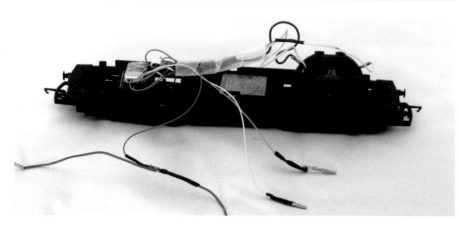

LEFT: *The decoder is held in place with some double-sided tape whilst a short length of spiral cable wrap keeps the wires under control. There is plenty of space in the body so there is no need to trim the cables back.*

The cut wires were connected to the red, black, orange and grey wires of the decoder. First a length of heat-shrink sleeving was slid onto the thicker of the two wires. Then the stripped lengths of the wires were twisted together. I soldered the wires together, straightened them out and pushed the heat-shrink sleeving into place. Holding the soldering iron by the sleeving makes it shrink and provide a snug insulated coating over the exposed wires, avoiding any possibility of them shorting against each other in the future.

The bogies were clipped back into the chassis and then the red decoder wire was connected to the trailing bogie, the black wire to the pick-ups on the motor bogie, the grey wire to the outer motor terminal and the orange wire to the inner motor terminal. The chassis was placed on the test track and power applied. Success – the chassis moved and went in the right direction – if it hadn't then it would have been a simple matter to swap the two motor connections over.

Next I turned my attention to the lighting. A bulb is located behind the headcode at each end, the one in the direction of travel being illuminated. The original wiring was discarded, but the four plugs for the bulbs were cut off and kept. The two diodes that controlled the directional lighting on DC were cut off and lobbed in the spares box. With DCC the lights get full voltage all the time; this makes them shine too brightly and could shorten their life considerably. I put a 100 Ohm resistor into the circuit to give more of a yellow glow rather than a bright white. One end of the resistor was soldered to the end of the decoder's blue wire, the common wire for all the function outputs, the other end was soldered to two wires with plugs for the bulbs on the other end. Plugs for the bulbs were soldered to the decoder's white and yellow wires. No extra components are needed as the directional lighting will be managed by the decoder.

Before the glazing unit went back on I used a length of spiral cable wrap to tidy up the wires inside the body. As there is plenty of space in there, there is no

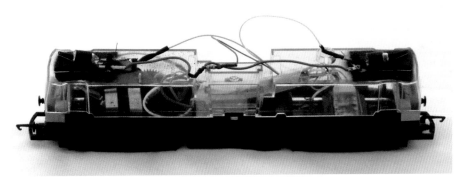

A 100 ohm resistor has been soldered to the lighting common wire to give the bulbs a yellow glow rather than a bright white beam, more in keeping with a diesel headcode. By re-using the Hornby connectors everything can be dis-assembled in the future if necessary.

As dusk falls on the railway the illuminated headcode is shown to advantage.

need to trim the wires back – useful if you ever want to take the decoder out and use it elsewhere. The decoder was fixed over the trailing bogie using some double-sided tape.

With the glazing reinstalled the lights were reconnected – yellow wire to the motor bogie end, white wire to the other end and one green wire to each end. Another test showed that my luck had held and I had got the wires the right way around – again if the wrong light comes on just swap the connections over.

Finally I put the body back on and then set the decoder's new address on the programming track before letting the locomotive loose on the layout. Whilst its slow speed performance is nowhere as good as my Bachmann Class 25s, it is adequate and an improvement on its behaviour before conversion. With further adjustment of the decoder settings I'm sure it could be improved further if necessary. Whilst the model was in bits I noticed that Hornby had made provision for fitting a smoke generator. Now, that decoder has two spare function outputs....

Dealing with the other type of Hornby Ringfield motor bogie

Motor bogies that have two screws at the top of the brush holders need more extensive work. Some motors have two connections to pickups, others only have one. In both cases there is a hidden connection that enables the motor to collect power from one side of the motor bogie. If you fail to disconnect this then your decoder will be destroyed the first time that you try to use it.

Looking at the motor bogie below there are two screws which keep the brush holders in place. The one on the right is perfectly normal, but the one on the left is longer and connects the brush holder to the chassis and thence to the track.

First you must remove the left hand screw. You need a solder tag and insulating washer to fit. Connect the solder tag to the decoder's black wire (track pick up). If the left hand brush retainer is also connected to a wire then that wire needs to be unsoldered and connected to the decoder's black wire. Now unsolder the other pick up from the right hand brush holder and connect to the decoder's red wire.

The grey wire can now be soldered to the left hand brush holder and the orange wire to the right hand one. Place the solder tag on the screw, followed by the insulating washer and then replace the screw. Make sure that the solder tag does not make contact with the brush holder or the chassis.

You can either make your own solder tags from brass strip or purchase them from Maplin Electronics, Rapid Electronics or Squires Model & Craft Tools. Similarly plastic sheet can be used to make suitable insulating washers, and can be shaped to ensure there is no possibility of the solder tag touching the motor or you can purchase them from Rapid Electronics or Squires Model & Craft Tools.

Looking at the motor bogie below, there are two screws which keep the brush holders in place. The one on the right is perfectly normal, but the one on the left is longer and connects the brush holder to the chassis and thence to the track.

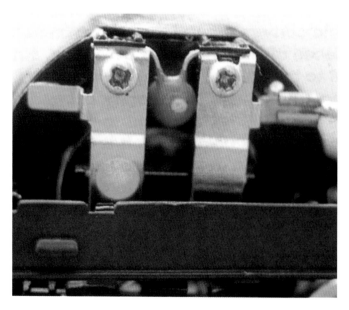

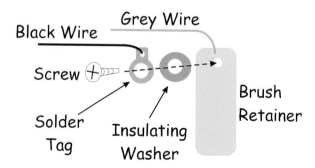

Above: *Connect the solder tag to the decoder's black wire (track pick up). Unsolder the other pick-up from the right hand brush holder and connect to the decoder's red wire. Solder the grey wire to the left hand brush holder and the orange wire to the right hand one. Place the solder tag on the screw, followed by the insulating washer and then replace the screw. Make sure that the solder tag does not make contact with the brush holder or the chassis.*

Hornby Class 121 Railcar

When people list the benefits of DCC over conventional analogue control you can bet that not far down the list *locomotive lights* will appear. The only problem is that there are an awful lot of locomotives that, despite being *DCC ready*, have no provision for lighting. So, as an example, here is a guide to fitting lights to the Hornby Class 121 Railcar.

The Hornby model is a re-issue of an earlier Lima product, now with flush glazing and a new motor bogie that features a DCC socket. Express Models provide a lighting kit for the old Lima model which is, needless to say, perfect for the Hornby one too. In addition you will need a suitable DCC decoder that provides directional lighting control (Function 0) – in this case I have used a Bachmann example but just about any decoder with an 8-pin plug would do.

The component parts for this project: Hornby Class 121 Railcar, a Bachmann DCC decoder with 8-pin socket and the Express Models lighting kit.

Once you have tested that the model works on DC, the first step is to get the body separated from the chassis. There are two large screws in the chassis that need to be undone after which you can gently lever the body off the chassis. Remove the DCC blanking plug, plug in the decoder and check that everything works. Establish which direction is forward – this is important when it comes to fitting directional lighting.

With the decoder plugged in we can test the model and establish which end is the 'front' – an important consideration when installing directional lighting.

Now we start on the tricky bit. Hornby fix their glazing in place with copious quantities of adhesive so there is no way that you are going to be able to get the moulded lights out of their housing without a bit of brute force. You need to drill the clear moulding out of the lights. First drill a small pilot hole through the centre of the lamp and then open it out with a 2mm diameter drill. Take it slowly and carefully. The pilot hole will keep the bigger drill on course and stop it wandering. You need to drill out the two lamps at each end.

As the glazing is firmly fixed in place you also need to drill out behind the lamps, using a much bigger drill, to allow the LEDs in the kit to fit in place. On the Lima model the glazing came out easily so the kit is designed to fit flush against the front of the model. You need to drill a 5mm hole through the glazing but not the front wall. If you don't do this then your lights will be recessed deep in the holes and will look very silly.

Using a pin-chuck and small drills you need to drill out the clear plastic mouldings from the lamps at the ends of the railcar.

Inside the model you need to drill a large clearance hole so that the LEDs in the lighting kit can fit flush against the front of the model.

You can remove the lip at the end of the chassis using a pair of pliers. This will provide space for the lighting board.

The front of the chassis unit needs to be cut away in order to accommodate the lighting board. To do this it is best to remove the seating unit by unclipping it from the chassis. You can remove the front lip at both ends of the chassis by simply pulling it away with a pair of pliers.

The cab area will need to be cut away from the seating unit to provide space for the lighting board. Once the seating unit is back in place you can push the LEDs into the holes that you drilled earlier and test fit the body. Work on one end at a time until both ends fit freely and easily.

At one end you will need to cut away part of the interior to make space for the lighting board. Test fit as you go, one end at a time, until everything fits easily.

Next you need to cut the white, blue and yellow wires as close to the plug as possible. Make sure that you cut the right wires and not at the decoder end – if you get it wrong you'll need a new decoder. Cut three lengths of heat shrink tubing and slip it over the three wires. Use wire strippers to remove about 1cm of insulation from each wire and from the white, blue and yellow wires attached to the lighting unit. Twist the pairs of wires together (white to white, etc.) and slide the tubing over the bare wire. Plug the decoder back in and you are ready to test the lights.

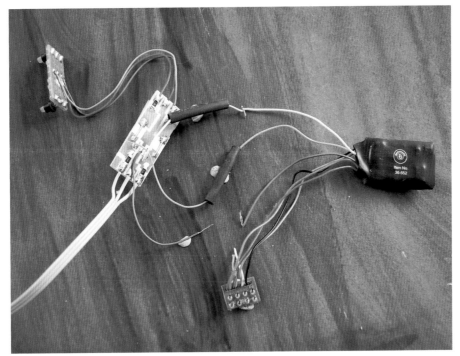

Cut the wires for the lights away from the plug and connect them to the lighting unit. Once the wires are soldered together the black heat shrink tubing will be used to insulate the bare wires.

Place the chassis on the track and fix the decoder, lighting board and lights down with Blu-Tack; this will stop any short circuits being caused by anything touching something that it shouldn't. Select the railcar on your controller and press Function 0 to switch the lights on. One pair should light up yellow, the other red. Now change the locomotive's direction (whilst still stationary) and the lights should swap over. Make a note as to which pair of lights is yellow when the railcar is set to go forward – these will go in the leading end. Switch off, unplug the decoder and put your soldering iron on to warm up.

Solder the wires together, slide the heat shrink tubing over the join and heat it with the side of the soldering iron. The tubing will shrink and make a tight sleeve covering the bare wires. Use a small amount of adhesive to fix the lights to each end of the railcar and fix the lighting board and decoder to the roof of the unit with sticky pads.

Plug the decoder in and replace the body, making sure that you don't trap any wires. Put the screws back in, place the railcar on the track and it is ready to go.

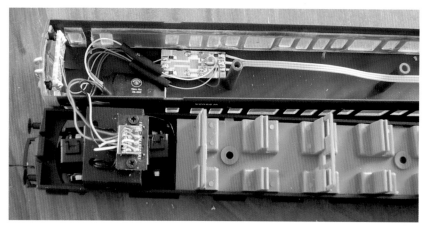

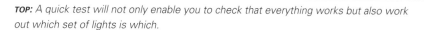

TOP: *A quick test will not only enable you to check that everything works but also work out which set of lights is which.*

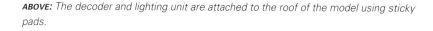

ABOVE: *The decoder and lighting unit are attached to the roof of the model using sticky pads.*

ABOVE: *Let there be light. The board on which the lights are mounted can be seen through the windscreen, but is not as obtrusive in reality as it appears in this photo. Some waste plastic from the drilling is still on the inside of the windscreen – looks like the body will have to come off again.*

Accessory Decoders

DCC can be used to control all sorts of accessories, from point motors to container cranes. This operating crane is a Heljan product seen on Nick Gurney's OO gauge Holland Park Container Terminal layout.

In this chapter we shall have a look at DCC Accessory Decoders. The idea is simple; you use the same DCC system to control your points, signals, level crossing gates and beer-drinking animated locals outside the model pub as you do for your locomotives.

The main stumbling block is cost. Many layouts don't have motorised points anyway and if you do then finding an extra £5 to £10 per point to cover the cost of a decoder is a pretty strong disincentive. So why bother?

- You don't need a control panel – having got rid of all those section switches you can now get rid of the switches for points and other accessories and dispense with the control panel altogether. This not only saves on space but also the cost of switches and all the wiring from the panel to the point motors.
- You can operate everything from your DCC handset. This is really useful when you are following your train around the layout – no need to dive back to the control panel to change a point.
- A computer can operate for you. Many DCC systems have computer interfaces and a PC can be used to automate sections, such as the fiddle yard, fill in for missing operators or run the mainline traffic whilst you shunt the yard.

Let's look at the types of accessory that are typically operated by DCC accessory decoders, and how to connect them.

Twin Coil Solenoid Point Motors

The typical model railway point motor consists of a pair of solenoid coils which need a pulse of electricity to operate them. If they are subjected to a continuous voltage they very quickly burn out.

Most accessory decoders are set to operate this type of point motor as a default.

One output is connected to each coil and the common wire is connected to both coils. This is exactly the same method as would be used for conventional operation with push buttons or similar switches. If your point motor has an auxiliary switch and your decoder has a feedback facility the switch can be connected to the decoder so that the point's setting can be read by the command station.

Where two point motors need to be operated at the same time, for example on a crossover, you should not connect both point motors to the same decoder output. Instead you should connect each point motor to its own individual output and set them both to the same address.

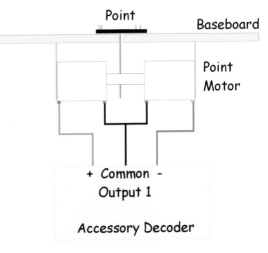

Point
Baseboard
Point Motor
+ Common -
Output 1
Accessory Decoder

Slow Motion Motors

Slow motion point motors such as the Tortoise or those produced by Fulgurex need to be connected differently to the twin solenoid types. They require a constant DC voltage in one direction or the other to operate and hold the point blades in position.

For DC output decoders you need to purchase an extra interface unit that converts the three-wire output to a two-wire one suitable for driving the motors.

For AC output decoders, such as the Lenz LS150 the interface consists of two standard diodes connected to route opposing polarities to one terminal of the point motor. The other terminal is connected to the common output of the decoder.

BELOW: A two-aspect colour light signal connected to an accessory decoder.

BOTTOM: Running an LED signal from an accessory decoder.

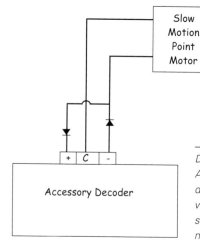

Decoders with an AC output need two diodes in the output wires to operate slow-motion point motors.

Colour Light Signals

Two-aspect colour light signals with 12V bulbs can be connected directly to the outputs of the accessory decoder.

Signals that use LEDs need a current-limiting resistor in order to work properly. Note also that the LEDs need to have the anodes connected together and to the common terminal on the decoder. Current flows from the common terminal through the LED to the + or – terminal. If you use LEDs on an AC ouput decoder (such as the Lenz LS150) you will also need to add a normal diode between the signal and the resistor (with the anode at the resistor end and the cathode at the signal end) to protect the LEDs from the AC voltage.

For a supply voltage of 16V AC the resistor should typically be 1K5Ω rated at 0.25W or greater. If your supply voltage is lower the LEDs may appear dim and in that case the resistor can be reduced to 1KΩ. If the LEDs are too bright for your needs then they can be dimmed by using a higher value resistor, normally 1K8Ω or 2K2Ω.

Multiple-aspect colour light signals cannot be directly operated using an accessory decoder but this accords with prototype practice, as on real railways the signals cycle through the different aspects automatically. The signalman can set a signal to red to stop a train and then clear the signal but the actual aspect that it displays (green, double yellow or yellow) is dependent on the position of other trains on the line.

If you have a multiple-aspect colour light system installed then the accessory decoder can act as the signalman's set/clear switch replacing the equivalent control on your signalling panel. To do this it will probably be necessary to connect a relay to the accessory decoder and use the relay contacts to replace the mechanical switch.

Other Accessories

You can, of course, use an accessory decoder to control just about anything that you would normally operate with a switch. Roco and Heljan produce DCC-operated cranes and it is easy to connect up lights, level crossings and other animated scenes.

A Selection of Accessory Decoders

Different accessory decoders have different facilities and it is a good idea to think about what you would like from your decoders before you purchase. You can, of course, mix and match using different decoders for different jobs if you wish. In this brief survey I shall look at four different types.

The Hornby R8216 is the cheapest of the readily available, ready to use units and is the most basic. It takes both the DCC signal and its power from the track or power bus. This means that when points are operated the power that they use is taken from the track power used for running trains which, on a large layout, could cause problems with the power supply being unable to cope. Not surprisingly it is only designed to operate twin-solenoid point motors. There is no option to vary the pulse length to help it throw sticky point motors and for programming it needs to be the only accessory decoder attached to the track or power bus. The accessory addresses are set in groups of 4.

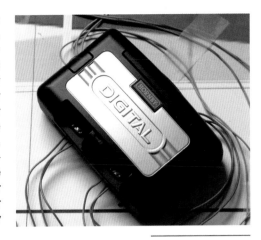

The Hornby R8216 Accessory Decoder has plastic covers that slot in to conceal the screw terminals.

The Lenz LS150 appears to be better value than some decoders by virtue of being able to operate six accessories rather than four. It can also operate a mixture of twin-solenoid and slow-motion (Tortoise or similar) point motors. The LS150 requires an extra 16V AC power supply as it only takes the DCC information from the track or power bus – it takes the power to operate the accessories from the separate power supply. This means that however many points you operate your locomotives will be unaffected. In passing the ideal power supply for this purpose is a discarded laptop computer power supply. These typically supply a well-regulated voltage with a capacity of around 4A. They can frequently be picked up free from someone whose laptop has expired. The pulse length can be varied to overcome awkward point motors but the decoder can have difficulty with some Peco point motors, especially older ones where the insulation has started to break down. Typically this will result in outputs shutting down as part of the unit's overload protection. In cases like these the decoder will need some extra help in the form of an external unit such as the DCC Concepts MasterSwitch which will act as a capacitor discharge unit. The output addresses can be set as a block of six or, if you prefer, individually. It is possible to wire in switches to operate the outputs manually, this may be useful in locations where a lot of shunting can take place, saving the effort of switching back and forth between point and locomotive control on the DCC handset. A button on the decoder selects programming mode, so it can be programmed in place without having to mess around disconnecting other decoders or running jump wires from the DCC controller to the unit.

The Lenz LS150 can control six point motors; most accessory decoders can only control four.

The Digitrax DS64 offers a lot of flexibility in installation and operation.

The Digitrax DS64 is the most expensive of the units examined but is the best specified. The four outputs can be configured to operate dual-solenoid or slow-motion point motors – but only one type for all four outputs. It can take its DCC information either from the track/power bus or by plugging in to the Digitrax LocoNet. The power for the accessories is 12V DC either from an accessory bus or a plug-in transformer.

The output addresses can be set as a group of four or individually. An additional feature is that you can set addresses to be part of a route. A route can consist of up to eight points that are all set from a single command. External switches can be used to operate outputs or routes manually. Like the Lenz unit a button on the decoder selects programming mode.

The final unit is a kit rather than ready-built. MERG (Model Electronic Railway Group) provide a range of kits for their members including two for DCC accessory decoders, one for dual-solenoid point motors and another for slow-motion motors. Whilst you do have to solder the components in place yourself, the process is quite straightforward and the instructions are clear and easy to follow. If you have a need for more than two decoders then it is well worth considering joining MERG and building your own. The output addresses are set as a group of four and the decoder needs to be the only one connected to the DCC controller for programming.

	Hornby R8216	Lenz LS150	Digitrax DS64	MERG Accessory Decoder
Size (approx)	10.5cm x 7cm x 3.5cm	12cm x 6cm x 2cm	12cm x 8.5cm x 3.5cm	9.5cm x 7.5cm
Fixings	Slots over 2 screws (supplied)	Two screw holes	Three screw holes	Four screw holes
DCC signal input	Track/power bus	Track/power bus	Track/power bus LocoNet	Track/power bus
Power input	With DCC signal	Separate 16V AC input	Track/power bus 12V DC input (bus or auxiliary power supply)	Separate 16V AC input
Types of point motor	Dual solenoid	Dual Solenoid Slow motion	Dual Solenoid Slow Motion (requires two additional diodes)	Dual solenoid or slow motion (different kits)
Can different types be mixed	No	Yes	No	No
Number of outputs	4	6	4	4
Independently addressed outputs	No	Yes	Yes	No
Manual operation possible?	No	Individual outputs can be activated by external push buttons	Individual outputs or routes can be activated by external switches	No
Programming	Must be the only accessory decoder connected to the track/power bus.	Programming mode is set using a button on the decoder	Programming mode is set using a button on the decoder	Must be the only accessory decoder connected to the track/power bus
Configuration options	None	Pulse duration	Solenoid or slow-motion operation. Pulse duration. Power-up options	Pulse duration

Wiring for DCC

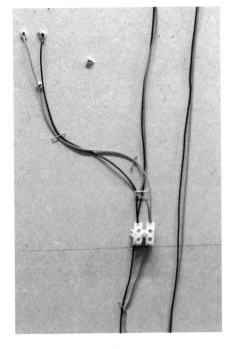

In the introduction I touched on the marketing myth that you just need two wires for DCC. Whilst this does have some truth in it, it is likely that you will need more than that – but a lot less than a conventional analogue DC layout. If you already have your layout wired up then it is possible to use that wiring but you may find it beneficial to rewire it. This can, of course, be done in stages over time.

The two most important wires on a DCC layout are usually called the track bus. These are the 'two wires' of mythology. Their job is to distribute the power and DCC signal to the track and anything else that happens to be connected to them.

These should be of thick cable to minimise any loss of power and should, as far as possible, run parallel to each other. Usually they are coloured red and black for easy identification. The track bus is connected to the track by short, thinner wires. Ideally each piece of rail should be connected to one of the bus wires but, as a minimum, the bus wires should be connected to the track at intervals of three to six feet. The table below gives the minimum recommended sizes for bus wires. If you have long wires, in excess of 4m, then you will need to use thicker cable to avoid the track voltage dropping as you get further away from the booster.

BELOW: Self-adhesive copper tape can be used for the bus wires in place of conventional wires. Track and accessory feeds can be soldered directly to the copper tape.

ABOVE: DCC wiring at its simplest. Here we have two pairs of bus wires with one set connecting to the track. If you have more than one bus, always keep their wires separate to avoid mistakes.

Booster Capacity	Bus Cable Size
3A bus	Single core wire – 20AWG
	Stranded wire – 16/0.2mm
	Conductor area (stranded or single core) - 0.5mm2
6A bus	Single core wire – 18AWG
	Stranded wire – 24/0.2mm
	Conductor area (stranded or single core) - 0.75mm2
10A bus	Stranded wire – 32/0.2mm
	Conductor area (stranded or single core) - 1.0mm2

As an alternative to wire you can use self-adhesive copper tape to carry the DCC power around your layout. The tape is sold for wiring dolls' houses and can be fixed to either the top or, more usually, the underside of the baseboard. As you only need two bus wires copper tape is a viable option – it wouldn't be suitable for analogue DC where there may be dozens of wires serving the same purpose. Track feeder wires and links to accessory decoders can be soldered to the tape and make the short run to their destination.

Incidentally it is recommended that DCC is not used for pickup from overhead wires unless both rails are electrically linked. If the overhead was connected to one of the running rails then turning a locomotive around, either manually or by running around a reverse loop, would cause a short circuit. In addition electrical pickup from an overhead wire tends to be far more erratic than from the rails, which can lead to unreadable DCC signals and the decoder losing power.

It is important to use sufficiently large wires for the track bus as it carries the current to run all the locomotives and accessories that are in use on the

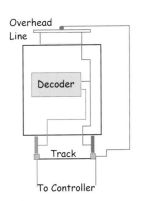

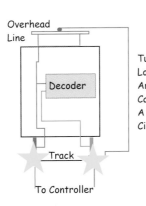

Overhead Line — Decoder — Track — To Controller

Overhead Line — Decoder — Track — To Controller — Turning Locomotive Around Causes A Short Circuit

LEFT: Using overhead catenary can cause short circuits if the locomotive also picks up from both rails. If the locomotive only picks up from one rail (the blue rail in the left hand illustration) then turning it round will leave it unpowered.

layout. Whilst thin wires may have no trouble with the 0.5A or so consumed by a modern OO gauge locomotive they will struggle with the demands of several sound-equipped locomotives and coach lighting. When a short circuit occurs on the layout, for example when a locomotive derails, then the full current from the booster will flow along the bus and through the short. As this will typically be between 2 and 5 Amps the booster is fitted with a high speed circuit breaker that detects the sudden current surge and shuts the power off thus preventing any damage to the booster, wiring or locomotives. However if the bus wires are too thin they can cause the track voltage to drop to such an extent that the booster cannot detect the short circuit and activate the circuit breaker. If that happens and the short is not removed, or the power shut off manually, the short can generate sufficient heat to damage track and rolling stock or even start a fire. You can test if your wiring is good enough to allow the booster to detect a short simply by placing something metal, such as a screwdriver, across the tracks at various places around the layout. The booster should shut down and indicate a short circuit every time. If it doesn't then you will need to increase the size of the bus wires or add extra feeds in the areas where short circuits are not detected.

Inadequate wiring also causes poor performance. Nickel-silver rail has a much higher electrical resistance than copper wire and if there are long runs without feeders from the track bus there will be a significant drop in the voltage at the track. This will cause locomotives to run slowly or even stop as the locomotive's decoder will shut down if there isn't enough power to operate it. This is particularly noticeable if you have locomotives with additional functions such as lights and sound.

Power Districts

Once you start using DCC you will quickly find that short circuits seem to happen more often than they did when you used DC and that when they happen they shut the whole system down. As a result many people believe that DCC is unreliable. So what causes this, and what can be done to avoid it?

With DCC all the track is live all the time. On DC track is only live when a locomotive is actually moving. With DC when you put a locomotive on the track, the controller is off. With DCC when you put a locomotive on the track it is live – so it is easy to short the rails together as you do it. Similarly if your locomotive wheels are not set to the correct gauge, not uncommon with ready-to-run stock, they can cause a short as they run through points. DC controllers tend to have slow-acting thermal overload cut-outs to protect them from short circuits, so a momentary short, such as a locomotive crossing a point, doesn't trip the cut-out and the locomotive's momentum carries it across the point and clears the short. The observer may see a spark, or the locomotive stutter, but will not register it as a short circuit. With DCC the electronic cut-out responds to a short very quickly and shuts down the power to the whole layout bringing not only the locomotive, but everything else, to a halt. You can minimise the problem of short circuits with DCC by checking that the metal wheels on locomotives and rolling stock are to the correct gauge and don't foul your points.

The other main cause of the system shutting down is driving a locomotive into a point that is set against it. Whilst the simple answer is that real locomotive drivers don't do it – so neither should you, mistakes do happen. The easy way to solve the problem is to change the point but if you are operating your points by DCC you can't do that until the short is cleared. What you need is a separate DCC circuit for the points.

Enter the power district. A power district is an area of the layout, be it track, points or accessories, which has an independent cut-out and, in some cases, their own power supply. Taking a simple end-to end layout as an example, it could either be station to station or station to fiddle yard. This can be divided into three power districts, one for each station plus half of the connecting line and one for the points, signals and other accessories. This would mean than a derailment or problem in the fiddle yard wouldn't stop operations in the station, and no matter what happens above the baseboard the points and signals would still work.

A power district does not need to be physically linked, for example on a double track oval with a fiddle yard to the rear, station to the front with a locomotive yard on one side of the station and goods yard to the other the power districts could be set up as:

1. Fiddle yard
2. Main lines and platforms
3. Goods yard and locomotive Yard.

You can purchase special units that divide the output from your DCC controller up into power districts. The units provide a number of outputs, each with its own electronic cut-out that will operate before the cut-out on the DCC controller, thus limiting the effect of a short circuit or overload to the district in which the problem has occurred. One such unit is the NCE EB3 Circuit Breaker. The EB3 provides short circuit protection for up to three power districts. If you need more than three power districts you can simply add more EB3's to the output of your DCC controller. The trip current and time can be set individually for each power district. This can be very useful if you are operating sound equipped locomotives as they tend to draw more current when they power up and a crowded diesel depot would benefit from some extra time or current when you turn your DCC system on. The EB3 has LEDs that indicate that all is well, or unwell, with each district. If you are a neat worker with a soldering iron you can add wires to extra LEDs mounted on your control panel. The EB3 can be used with any manufacturer's DCC system.

The EB3 comes with screw terminals for the wires to and from the controller and track, so no soldering is necessary in order to install it. Using the small plastic connectors supplied you can set each power district to limit the current to 2, 3 or 4 Amps. To adjust the time before a power district shuts down when a short is encountered you need a DCC system that can program locomotives on the main line. The response time can be varied for each power district from 1/100th of a second up to half a second. As supplied the unit is set at 1/10th of a second.

Installation is simple and the unit can be mounted under the baseboard. The board has four mounting holes. The manufactures recommend using no.4 x ¾" (19mm) round head wood screws with no.4 flat washers. Do not over tighten the screws. Lightly snug the screws up just enough to keep the circuit board in place without bending it. Bending the circuit board can fracture the fragile electronic components. I covered the washers with adhesive tape to ensure that the did not accidentally bridge any contacts on the circuit board. Connect up the input wires to your DCC controller and the output wires to the track (don't forget to isolate the power districts from each other, either by cutting gaps in both rails or fitting

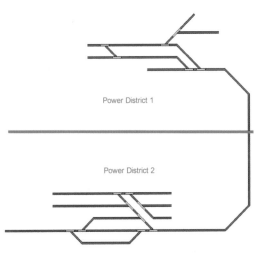

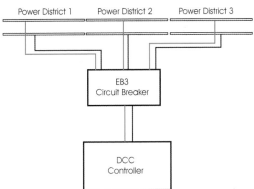

An NCE EB3 circuit breaker. The wires on the left are connected to the DCC command station, the wires on the right are the track bus for three separate sections of the layout.

TOP: By dividing this layout into two power districts a problem at one station won't affect operations at the other.

ABOVE: A circuit breaker allows the layout to be divided into separate electrical sections.

insulating rail joiners) and you are ready to go. You can test the unit is working correctly by shorting the track in each power district – put a coin across the rails. If everything is connected up correctly your DCC controller should still be operational and one of the LEDs on the EB3 will flash.

One thing to watch for if you are installing power districts is to ensure that you are consistent with connecting the red and black bus wires in each section. The easiest way to check that you have done this correctly is to use a meter set to its AC Volt scale and connect it to the 'red' rail in two different sections. If the meter reads 0V then both rails really are 'red'. If it reads the full DCC voltage (around 14V) then one rail is 'red' and the other 'black'. Swap the connections over in one of the sections and try again.

If you operate point motors and other accessories using DCC you may wish to have a separate bus for them to avoid their current draw affecting the trains. Another possibility is to use point motor decoders that have their own capacitor discharge unit (CDU) which will provide the large kick that solenoid point motors need to operate without leaving the rest of the layout short of power.

Trouble-shooting Sections

Regardless of the number of power districts that you have installed you will find it really useful to add a number of switches along each track bus to turn off sections of track for trouble-shooting purposes. It is far easier to locate a short circuit if you can work out roughly where it is. The track connected to each section of the bus will need to be isolated from the other track sections on both rails for the switches to work.

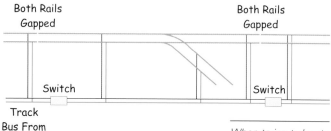

Both Rails Gapped · Both Rails Gapped · Switch · Switch · Track Bus From Booster

When trying to locate a short circuit you can turn the switches off one by one, working back towards the booster, until the short circuit clears. This tells you that the short circuit is in the section controlled by the last switch that you turned off. Using the diagram above as an example, suppose that there is a locomotive causing a short circuit at the point. Turning off the right hand switch would not clear the short. Turning off the left hand switch would. From this you would know that the short was in the centre section of the track and could quickly home in on the problem.

Reverse Loops and Wyes

Reverse loops and their relation the wye are one of the nightmares of model railway wiring. For those using clockwork, live-steam, battery power or even old three-rail track they are not a problem and can be scattered about the layout like confetti, but for those of us who use conventional 2-rail wiring, both DC and DCC, they are a problem.

If you have a reverse loop on your layout then at some point a rail connected to the 'red' power bus will meet a rail connected to the 'black; power bus and a short circuit will be created.

The same thing happens where you have a wye configuration. These can sometimes be found where a branch comes off a continuous run.

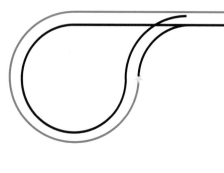

When you have a reverse loop or wye configuration no matter how you arrange things sooner or later a 'red' powered rail will meet a 'black' powered rail and cause a short. Whilst placing insulating rail joiners somewhere on the loop will solve the short, you won't actually be able to run anything around the loop because as soon as a metal wheel crosses the join the short will reappear as the two sides are connected through the wheel or locomotive.

With DC controllers the normal solution is to feed the loop through a switch that can reverse the power connections to the rails. In operation you set the switch one way, run the train into the loop and stop, throw the switch, reverse the direction switch on the controller and then bring the train out of the other end of the loop. Your locomotive is now facing the other way when the controller is set to 'forwards'. Some people use a switch linked to the point motor or point lever at the entrance to the loop to ensure that the power is set correctly for the direction chosen. This has the advantage that you won't get a sudden short if the power switch is set the wrong way for a train moving into or out of the loop, but can have an interesting effect if the point is changed whilst the train is in motion as the locomotive will suddenly change direction.

With DCC controllers we still have the 'red' rail meeting 'black' rail problem and, unless you are using power districts you will bring the entire railway, and quite possibly point operation, to a halt. The good news is that the switch method still works with DCC with the advantage that as locomotive direction is controlled by the

Points and Crossings

Despite the many myths and misinformation to the contrary there is no fundamental difference in wiring up points for DCC. The only thing to remember is that with DCC all rails that have power fed into them are always live whereas with analogue DC the power could be switched off.

The illustrations below all show live frog points. As with analogue DC live frog points ensure electrical contact for the locomotive and make for smoother running. Peco Streamline 'electrofrog' points can be laid in exactly the same way as dead, or insulated, frog points with no extra wiring. Most other brands require the frog and associated rails to be electrically switched when the point is changed. This can be done by a switch linked to the point motor or lever.

The secret with any pointwork is to always feed electrical power from the toe of the points. One feed can run through a number of points as long as they all face in the same direction, or to put it another way, when coming from the feed you should always pass the point blades before you get to the frog.

You will note that the turnouts retain their power switching function under DCC and that the sidings with the points set against them are electrically dead. This

means that any DCC-equipped locomotive on the isolated siding will not respond to the controller.

To make a siding live at all times you need to put insulating rail joiners on both rails after the frog and then run feeder wires to the siding. The siding will now be live at all times but you will be able to run a locomotive into a point that is set against it and cause a short circuit which will shut down the booster. This is the single most common cause of short circuits on DCC layouts.

Don't forget that there can be a long length of track between any of the points and that they can fan out in both directions from the feed.

Live frog points need the same frog switching wiring as they do for conventional DC analogue layouts. This is covered in detail in *Aspects of Modelling: Railway Electrics*. The other problem that can occur with points is when out-of-gauge wheelsets bridge the gap between the frog rails and running rails to cause a short or where locomotives with long rigid wheelbases are running around sharp curves. If you must do this then the point needs to be modified so that the blades are connected to the adjacent running rail and the frog is electrically switched by the point motor or lever. The instructions supplied with Peco points explain how to do this.

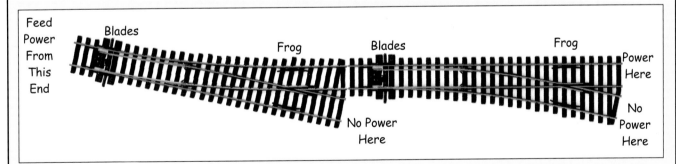

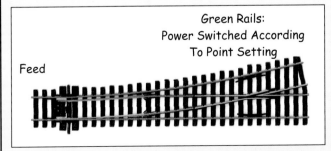

ABOVE: The secret with any pointwork is to always feed electrical power from the toe of the points. One feed can run through a number of points as long as they all face in the same direction.

LEFT: Peco Electrofrog points can be modified so that the blades are connected to the adjacent running rail and the frog is electrically switched by the point motor or lever.

on-board decoder your locomotive will still go forwards when you select forward on the controller. The disadvantage of using the switch system is that if you don't set it correctly you will get a short and, given the lack of switches needed with DCC it is easy to forget. If you are using sound decoders it is possible for the brief break in supply whilst you throw the switch to cause them to reset and you will need to turn the sound on again.

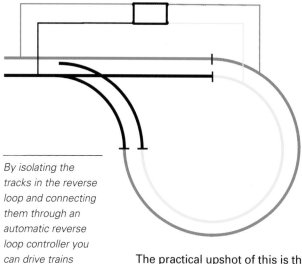

By isolating the tracks in the reverse loop and connecting them through an automatic reverse loop controller you can drive trains through the loop without worrying about short circuits. The controller will sort everything out for you.

A far more elegant solution is offered by the automatic reverse loop units available from various manufacturers. You can use any manufacturer's reverse loop unit, regardless of which DCC controller you have. These are, in essence, specialised versions of the power district units. When the reverse loop unit detects a short circuit instead of cutting the power it tries reversing the power connections, if the short circuit is still there then it cuts the power. This is achieved in a matter of thousandths of a second so the locomotive decoder doesn't notice the interruption to the power supply. The decoder doesn't care which rail is 'red' or 'black' so carries on doing whatever it was doing before the power connections were reversed.

The practical upshot of this is that you can drive a locomotive into a reverse loop that is connected to an automatic reverse loop unit without worrying about which way a switch is set, throw the point with the locomotive still moving and exit from the loop without slowing down. Alternatively you could run into the loop and then reverse out. The reversing loop becomes just like any other length of track as far as operation is concerned.

There are two restrictions: if you are using trains that pick up power along their length, for example multiple units that pick up from more than one carriage or lighted coaches, then the section of track connected to the automatic reversing loop unit must be longer than your longest train, otherwise the unit will shut down. (This restriction also applies to using a switch on DC.) The second restriction applies if you want to use DC locomotives on your DCC layout. Although the locomotive can be controlled by the DCC system, its direction still depends on the polarity of the DCC track voltage. Whilst the automatic unit will correctly set the power for the loop when the locomotive enters you still need a switch between the reversing unit and the loop. Stop the DC locomotive, throw the switch, reverse the direction on the controller and then drive it out, just like you would on DC.

The Bachmann 36-525 reverse loop controller has a switch to select the current draw which will trigger its operation.

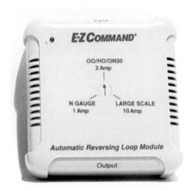

The Lenz LK100. As supplied, this unit comes set to recognise anything over 2A as a short-circuit. A small screwdriver operated dial on the side of the unit allows you to change this to between 1A and 10A depending on your needs.

Connecting one of these units is quite simple. First you put insulating rail joiners on both rails at both ends of the loop. The joiners need to be opposite each other, not staggered. Connect the tracks on the loop to the output from the unit and connect the DCC power bus to the input of the unit. On some units you need to select the power output you require using a switch. That's it, you are now ready to go.

First Use

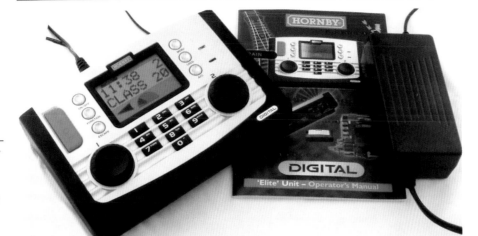

Having got your new DCC system out of the box, the first thing you need to do is read that instruction manual.

This is it. You've unpacked your command station and fitted a decoder to a locomotive. Now you can't wait to get started. So what should you do first?

Read the instructions. I know it sounds terribly dull but virtually all command station manuals include a 'quick start' or similar section that will give you enough information to set the system up and run a train without getting too frustrated or damaging anything.

Don't get carried away and start wiring your unit straight into your layout. The first thing to do is set up a section of programming track so that you can check your first locomotive conversion(s).

Following the instructions connect the various components together and connect the programming track outputs to a length of track. Turn the power on and check that the command station and cab show the correct lights and displays.

Take your first DCC converted locomotive and place it on the track. Following the instructions for your particular DCC system check that the decoder responds correctly. You can now set the locomotive address.

Now connect a second length of track, or ideally an oval, to the track terminals of your booster unit. Check that the track wiring is OK by placing a coin across the rails and seeing that the booster shuts down. Remove the coin and, if necessary, reset the booster. Now put your locomotive on the track and try driving it.

Once you have got the hang of driving your locomotive you might wish to experiment with changing CVs for start voltage, maximum speed, acceleration and deceleration to see how these affect the locomotive's behaviour (see Chapter 8: Advanced Use for more details). Once you have found settings that you like make a note of the locomotive's decoder type, address and CV settings for future reference.

Test a second locomotive on the programming track and then on the running track. Once you are happy with that locomotive place them both on the running track and experiment with running two locomotives at once, both individually and double-headed.

Connecting Up

Having got the hang of the system, you are now ready to connect it up to your layout.

Assuming that you are replacing one or more analogue controllers, your first task is to disconnect all the controllers. If you have a cab control system, where any controller can connect to any track section, you need to set all the cab switches to the same cab and connect the DCC system in place of that controller. If each of your analogue controllers is connected to a specific track section then you will need to connect the DCC system in place of all the controllers. Either way, don't forget to turn on any isolating sections used for holding locomotives.

Running Analogue Locomotives with DCC

Most DCC systems allow you to run a standard analogue locomotive on your DCC system. Whilst this is very useful you should be aware that analogue locomotives should not be left standing on powered track for more than a few minutes at a time.

Any analogue locomotive left standing on a DCC powered track will seem to buzz. This is due to the track voltage continuously changing between a positive voltage of around fourteen volts to a negative one, and back again. Whilst the average voltage seen by the motor is zero and thus the motor doesn't run, the constant changes of voltage do cause the motor to buzz and heat up. If the locomotive is left in this state for more than a few minutes the heat can cause the motor windings to melt and the motor to expire with a wisp of smoke. To avoid this you need to ensure that any analogue locomotive that is not in motion or temporarily stopped is either removed from the layout or parked on an isolated track.

To run analogue locomotives the DCC system stretches some of the pulses, either on the positive or negative cycle, depending on the direction of travel required. This changes the overall average voltage seen by the locomotive, whilst not affecting DCC operation. This means that the DC voltage seen by an analogue locomotive is pulsed rather than smooth DC. Whilst this can give better slow speed performance from some locomotives, the rapid pulsing will destroy high-quality coreless motors, such as the Escap range. These are normally only found in kit-built locomotives, but if you are in any doubt DO NOT run an analogue locomotive on DCC until you have checked that it is not fitted with a coreless motor.

Wire up the DCC command station/booster following the instructions and double-check your connections before you turn on the power.

Test that a short circuit on the track will cause the system to shut down by placing a screwdriver or coin across the track with the DCC system on. If the system does not shut down immediately you will need to improve your wiring – see chapter 6 *Wiring for DCC.*

Place a locomotive fitted with a decoder on the track, set its address on the controller and start driving.

If you encounter problems then consult the troubleshooting guide at the end of this book or the equivalent section in your command station manual.

One common problem is a short circuit caused by running up to a point that is set against the locomotive. The solution is not to do it – real engine drivers don't, so neither should you.

Replacing a cab control system with a DCC controller.

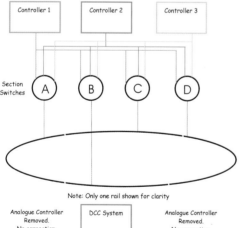

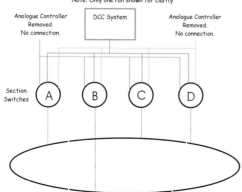

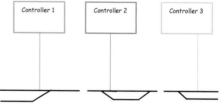

Replacing directly connected DC controllers with a DCC system.

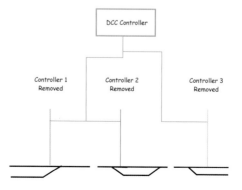

Programming Tracks

It is useful to have a programming track on your layout, but you will probably want it connected to the rest of the trackage so that you don't have to lift locomotives off the rails to change their CV settings. Even if your DCC system allows you to program 'on the main' you will find that in order to read the settings you will still need to use the programming track. If you have a simple system, such as the Bachmann E-Z controller, that does not have a separate programming track output, it is still useful to create a programming track to save you having to take all the other locomotives off the layout every time that you want to set a locomotive's address.

The diagram left shows how to convert a siding on your layout into a programming track using the programming track outputs from your DCC system.

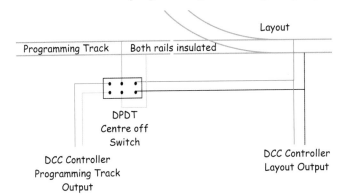

It is important that the DPDT switch is a centre off type so that there is no possibility of the programming and normal outputs of the controller being connected to the programming track at the same time. Both rails need to be electrically isolated from the main layout using insulated rail joiners.

In normal use the switch would be set to connect the siding to the layout and it would behave just like any other siding. To program a locomotive you need to drive it onto the siding. Make sure that the whole locomotive is in the siding and no wheels are on the layout side of the insulated gap. Change the switch to connect the siding to the programming output of the controller. You can now program the decoder. Once you have finished, change the switch to connect the siding back to the layout and drive the locomotive off the siding.

The diagram right shows how to convert a siding on your layout into a programming track for a simple system, such as the Bachmann E-Z controller, that does not have programming track outputs. The programming track will not add any extra functions to the controller but will enable you to change decoder addresses without having to remove locomotives from the layout. In this case the switch is a double-pole on/off switch.

In normal use the switch would be 'ON' so that power is fed to both the siding and the layout. To change a locomotive's address you need to drive it onto the siding. Make sure that the whole locomotive is in the siding and no wheels are on the layout side of the insulated gap. Change the switch to 'OFF'. The siding will still have power but the rest of the layout will no longer be connected to the

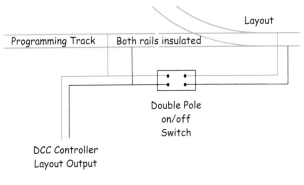

DCC system. You can now change the locomotive's address. Once you have finished change the switch back to 'ON' and drive the locomotive off the siding.

Three suggested suppliers of suitable switches are listed below:

DPDT centre off:			DPDT on/off		
Maplin Electronics Ltd.	part no.	*FH05F Sub-min Toggle F*	*Maplin Electronics Ltd.*	part no.	*FH04E Sub-min Toggle E*
Rapid Electronics Ltd.	part no.	*75-0145 DPDT Centre-off*	*Rapid Electronics Ltd.*	part no.	*75-0140 DPDT*
Squires Model & Craft Tools	part no.	*MT0080 Mini Toggle DPDT C/Off On-Off-On*	*Squires Model & Craft Tools*	part no.	*MT0070 Mini Toggle DPDT On-On*

CHAPTER

Advanced Use

Tailoring decoder performance will enable you to get the best out of each locomotive. Limiting the top speed of your shunting locomotives will give excellent slow speed control.

Tailoring Decoder Performance

When people are telling you about the advantages of DCC, one of the benefits that is quoted is that you can tailor the decoder settings to suit the locomotive. This sounds good, but what does it actually mean? In fact most people just set the locomotive's address and leave it at that. So what can you do, and how do you do it?

To make things easy you really need a DCC controller that can 'Program on the Main', as setting decoder CVs gets very tedious if you have to keep switching the locomotive from the layout to the programming track and back. Your controller needs to display the current speed step as well, as it saves a lot of guesswork. I shall assume that the locomotive address has already been set and you are ready to move on.

If you need to change the direction that the decoder regards as 'forwards' then you can set this using CV (Configuration Variable) 29. This CV controls a number of things, but the only one we are interested in here is the 'Direction of Travel'. On most systems the options are '0' (normal) or '1' (reverse). Simply change the setting from what it currently is, to the other one, save it and your locomotive will now move in the opposite direction when you select forwards.

Much of the tailoring process is involved with speed and acceleration so you need a continuous run of some form. If your layout provides one then all is well, otherwise you will have to sweep the kitchen floor and put down an oval of track.

Before we begin we have to establish how far one lap of the track is. You can either calculate this or measure it. An oval of second radius track with a double straight on each side measures 134in (3.4m) per lap and this is the dimension that I shall use for my example.

Now for the science bit. For OO, which has a scale of 1:76, a scale mile measures 1/76th of a real one, that is 1,760 yards, or 63,360 inches divided by 76. This comes to 834in (21.2m). For N gauge a scale mile is 428in (10.9m) and for O gauge it is 1,473in (37.4m). So an OO gauge train travelling at a scale 60 mph (which is a mile a minute) will cover a scale mile, or 834in (21.2m), in a minute or nearly 14in (355mm) (834/60) per second. On that basis the locomotive would lap my test oval once every 9.6 seconds. Now, if we work out the lap time for various speeds we can work out how fast the locomotive is going, and if we use the time for five laps rather than one we can stop worrying about tenths of a second and use an ordinary clock or watch for our timing.

So to calculate the lap time for a given speed and circuit length we do the following calculation:

Lap Time = (Circuit Length x 3,600) ÷ (Scale Speed x Scale Mile)

So for 90 mph we would calculate:

Circuit length x 3,600 = 134 x 3,600 = 482,400

Scale Speed x Scale Mile = 90 x 834 = 75,060

Lap Time = 482,400 ÷ 75,060 = 6.4 seconds

To get the time for five laps we simply multiply the circuit length by five before we start, giving us a five-lap time of 2412000 ÷ 75060 = 32 seconds.

A few minutes work with a calculator will give you a table of speeds and times for your test circuit. In my case they are:

Scale Speed (mph)	10	20	30	40	50	60	70	80	90	100
Five Laps Take (seconds)	289	145	96	72	58	48	41	36	32	29

Armed with this information we can now set the maximum speed of our locomotive.

The maximum speed is set by changing CV 5 (Vmax), Maximum Voltage. As most model locomotives go much faster than the real thing you will need to reduce the value in CV5 until the model's top speed is somewhere about right. Check your decoder documentation but usually CV 5 will have a default setting of 256 – try something around 160 to start with and increase or decrease it a little at a time. This is where programming on the main comes into its own, you can turn the controller right up, time five laps, stop, change the CV and then try again. Don't feel that you have to get the speed spot on, lives are not at stake here.

If you have a good decoder with back-EMF (feedback) you shouldn't need to adjust the start voltage (CV 2 - Vmin) – the locomotive should start to move on speed step 1 without any fiddling. However, if your locomotive refuses to move at low throttle settings increasing CV 2 a little at a time will get the locomotive to behave properly.

We now have a locomotive that will start to move when we open the throttle and will travel at a prototypical maximum speed when it is flat out. The next CV that we need to look at is CV 6 (Vmid), the mid-point. CV 6 sets the locomotive speed at the throttle's half-way setting. You can use this to get the best out of the locomotive for your layout. If it is a shunting locomotive you may wish to set CV 6 at less than half way between CV 2 (Vmin) and CV 5 (Vmax), this will mean that more of the controller's travel is at low speeds rather than high speeds, making the locomotive more controllable at slow speeds. Similarly if you only have a 6ft (1.8m) long shunting layout there is little scope for any locomotive to get up to its maximum speed, so reducing the value of CV 6 will be a benefit. If you are blessed with a long main line run you may still need to amend CV 6 to reflect any changes you have made to CV 2 and CV 5. For example if you have reduced CV 5 from 256 to 160 then the mid-point ought to be reduced to half of the CV 5 value, in this case 80. Be warned that if you reduce CV 5, the maximum speed, to a value that is less than CV 6, the mid-point, some decoders will behave strangely and make locomotives run away at top speed.

Now that we have got a nicely behaved locomotive we can look at acceleration and deceleration. Trains are not like cars, they take a while to build up speed, and even longer to stop. Very few layouts can cope with realistic braking rates, but we can simulate it using CV settings to stop the 'stops on a sixpence' behaviour you sometimes see.

CV 3 controls the acceleration rate and CV 4 controls the deceleration rate. Suitable values will depend on both your layout and the work that the locomotive will do. A shunting locomotive will only need a low value, accelerating and braking quickly. Locomotives hauling heavy freight trains will start and stop far more slowly and will require higher settings. Change them gradually – increasing or decreasing by 4 or 5 each time until you get a rate that suits you.

It will take you a little while to tweak the CV settings for each locomotive, but you only have to do it once – the decoder will remember the settings and use them every time that you run the locomotive. With the top speed restricted, slow speeds more responsive to the controller and trains that start and stop like the real thing I am sure that you will consider it time well spent.

CV	Description	Typical Default
CV 2	Minimum Speed (Vmin)	0
CV 3	Acceleration Rate	0
CV 4	Deceleration Rate	0
CV 5	Maximum Speed (Vmax)	256
CV 6	Mid-point Speed (Vmid)	0 (not set)

Please bear in mind that not all decoders support these CVs. Check your decoder manual.

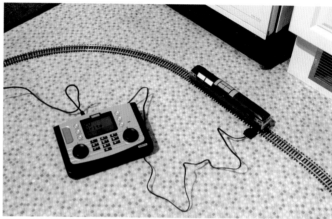

No one would expect a Jinty to behave like a Class 47 in real life. With DCC you can tailor the locomotive's decoder settings to make your model locomotives behave more like the real thing.

Double Heading

It may not be elegant, but if you only have an end to end layout an oval of track on a clean floor makes tailoring decoder settings a lot easier.

Another of the oft-quoted benefits of DCC is the ease with which double-heading can be performed. Double-heading is where two locomotives are used to haul a train and happened for a number of reasons on real railways.

The first is quite simply that the train was too heavy for one locomotive to move; the railways had far more small and medium sized locomotives than large ones so it was often necessary to use two smaller locomotives instead of a big one. Also a number of lines couldn't take the weight of a large freight or express locomotive so a pair of smaller locomotives would be used instead.

Sometimes it was operational needs that resulted in double-heading. A locomotive on its way to or from works attention could be added to a train rather than running light engine on a busy line. Similarly a failing or failed engine could be assisted by another. Where a train is diverted or routed over lines which the crew is not familiar with a pilot locomotive could be attached to the front driven by a local crew.

For modellers there is rarely any need to double-head our trains, as powerful motors and free-running rolling stock make it unnecessary; however, we do like to replicate prototype practice and anyway, a double-headed train looks good.

DCC offers at least three ways to double-head trains. The first is simply to set the decoders in both locomotives to the same address. The second is called universal consisting where the DCC controller sends the same control signals to two different locomotives. The third is advanced consisting where the locomotive decoder responds to both its own address and a second, consist, address. The terms 'consist' and 'consisting' come from the US, and refer to running a number of locomotives in multiple. In the US trains are regularly hauled by four or more locomotives – in the UK it is very rare to need more than two.

The way that consisting is implemented varies with different DCC controllers and decoders; not all features are available in all systems and those that are may behave differently from each other. The first port of call is the user manual, usually followed by a healthy dose of experimentation.

Simple Consisting

This is a term that I have just coined, to describe setting two (or more) locomotive decoders to the same address. It is very simple to set up but is not very flexible. It is best suited to locomotives that will always work together as a pair, such as a pair of Class 20 diesels. By placing the locomotives on the programming track individually the decoder settings can be modified as necessary, for example to set one locomotive to run backwards and the other forwards.

It is not possible to operate the locomotives individually, however this method will work with any DCC controller or locomotive decoder.

Universal Consisting

In universal consisting the donkey work is performed by the DCC controller. A locomotive address is allocated to the consist and when that address is selected the commands are sent to both the locomotives. Using the controller you can add and remove locomotives from the consist so it is possible to run the locomotives individually when you need to. This allows you to run a train headed by a single locomotive, pull into a station where a second locomotive is added to the front and then the train can depart double-headed.

Universal consisting is controlled entirely from the DCC controller. Some simple controllers, such as the Bachmann E-Z controller, do not support it whilst others have limited functionality. Usually the controller will have a limit to the number of consists and locomotives in each consist that it can handle, although this is not likely to be a problem on a British-outline layout.

As the consist information is in the controller, rather than the locomotive decoders, if you move the locomotives to a different layout or connect a different controller, then the consist information will need to be re-entered on the new controller.

Depending on the way that universal consisting has been implemented on your controller you may find that the consist can be controlled by both the consist's own address and also the individual locomotive addresses, or just the consist address.

Advanced Consisting

With advanced consisting the consist information is held in the locomotive decoders and this feature tends to be available in newer and more expensive designs. Some controllers directly support setting up advanced consists, whilst on others you have to set the necessary CVs yourself.

With advanced consisting the DCC controller sends commands to the consist address and these are picked up and actioned by all the locomotives in the consist. As the consist information is stored in the locomotive decoders the locomotives will still work together if they are moved to a different layout or a different controller is connected.

The locomotives in an advanced consist will not respond to speed or direction commands send to their own address – only the consist address. Decoder functions, such as lighting and sound, are a more complex area and it is possible to change their behaviour using CV settings. Normally the functions will only respond to instructions sent to the locomotive's address and not the consist address.

Matching Locomotives Up

Normally any two locomotives will behave differently. This is especially true given the way that DCC allows you to tailor the top speed, acceleration rate and other characteristics of each locomotive. For successful double-heading both locomotives need to be travelling at about the same speed at all times.

The easiest way to do this is to match the speeds of the locomotives that you are going to use by adjusting CVs 2 (Start Voltage), 5 (Top Speed) and 6 (Mid-range Speed) whilst running them around a circuit.

With universal and advanced consisting your DCC controller will normally have a means of selecting the direction of travel for each locomotive within the consist, so that no matter which way is normally forwards for each locomotive, they travel the same way when working as a pair. The usual method is to ensure that they are set to travel in the same direction when they are put in the consist.

Back-EMF

Back-EMF, or feedback, is a system used by a number of locomotive decoders to make locomotives run smoothly. In simple terms it checks the motor's speed, compares it to what it is supposed to be and adjusts the power to the motor accordingly. This keeps a locomotive at a constant speed whether it is going around a curve, straight and level, up or down hill. However different decoder manufacturers implement it in different ways. If the locomotives in your consist use decoders from different manufacturers you may find that you have to turn the Back-EMF option off to get them to work together reliably. This is also true if one decoder has Back-EMF and the other doesn't.

RIGHT: With DCC you can tailor individual locomotive's performance to reflect the real thing. This can cause problems when double-heading and you will need to adjust the decoder CV settings so that both locomotives run at the same speed. Different decoders and locomotive types need careful matching before putting them together in a consist. In this case a Bachmann Ivatt and Hornby Jinty have both been fitted with Lenz Silver decoders. The CV settings on the Jinty were adjusted so that its speed and acceleration matched the Ivatt.

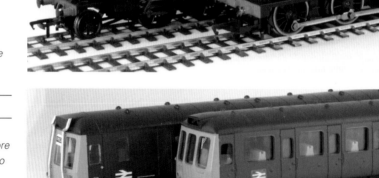

RIGHT: Diesel multiple units (DMUs) often worked together in formations of two or more units. Sometimes units would be attached to or detached from the formation during the course of the journey. This is the sort of prototype operation that is easy to replicate using DCC. The photo shows a Hornby Class 121 railcar and a Lima Class 117; these classes could often be found working together on the British Rail's Western Region.

RIGHT: Class 20s were usually seen in pairs coupled nose to nose with the cabs facing outwards. For DCC operation this means that one of them will have to be set up to run backwards when the other goes forwards.

*RIGHT: Double-heading in action. This photo shows Nos 45353 and 73134 passing Salford on a heavily loaded passenger working from Manchester Exchange to Llandudno Junction in the summer of 1963.
Photo: Author's collection*

Driving with Sound

Sound-equipped locomotives are one of the features that tends to convince people to use DCC rather than conventional control. Thanks to Bachmann and Hornby you can even buy locomotives ready-to-run with sound decoders installed which gives even those who have never fitted a decoder the opportunity to experience this development.

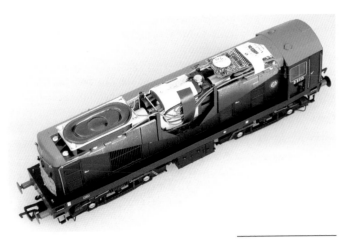

Sound decoders are, by their nature, at the expensive end of the decoder market, and as a result tend to come with the 'up-market' features that you expect in a top-end decoder. To those who are used to budget decoders this can be a big change, and even those who normally use a high-end decoder will find that driving a 'noisy' locomotive requires a different technique to a silent one.

This cutaway shows how the speaker is positioned inside Bachmann's Class 20 locomotive. Photo: Andy York

To get the best from a sound decoder you need to have a DCC controller that gives you easy access to functions 1 to 8 – or even higher, depending on the facilities that the particular decoder and collection of sounds offers. To demonstrate the way that sound can transform operation I shall be using the Bachmann Class 20 as an example.

The first thing to do is to make yourself a little crib sheet to refer to whilst operating as it is easy to forget which function does what. For the Class 20 the functions are:

F1 – Sound on/off	F5 – Buffer clang
F2 – Single horn	F6 – Coupling
F3 – Double horn	F7 – Shunt speed on/off
F4 – Air brake	F8 – Inertia on/off

Ready to start the day's work. We have a sleeping locomotive, a DCC controller and the vital crib sheet.

Once we have waited for the start-up sequence to finish we can crawl across the yard pointwork.

Our locomotive starts the shift sitting in a siding. The engine driver climbs in and starts it up. Press F1 and the locomotive splutters into life. You will notice that you cannot get the locomotive to move during the start up sequence, however much you try. So we simulate the driver checking the locomotive until it is ready to move.

It is not uncommon for drivers to give a quick toot on the horn before moving off, to warn anyone who is in the area to watch out for the moving locomotive. Pressing F2 gives a single tone. Here is the first trap for the unwary. Most DCC controllers toggle their function outputs, switching them on at the first press and off at the second. The sound decoder will only respond to the function being turned on, so for a noise like a horn you need to press the function button twice. Press once for the sound and then again once the sound has finished to turn the function off.

BELOW: As we nuzzle up to the train the buffers clash, courtesy of a quick press of F5.

If this is the first time that you have used a decoder with an inertia function you will wonder why the locomotive doesn't respond to the controller and will keep increasing the setting until the locomotive starts to move. You will then find it accelerating away despite your turning the control back down. When using inertia you need to set the controller to the speed you want and leave the locomotive to accelerate up to it. For shunting manoeuvres it can be very difficult to judge exactly the right place to stop so you can disable the inertia by pressing F8. There is an additional facility to reduce the maximum speed by half by pressing F7 which gives greater slow speed control when shunting. Some controllers, such as the Hornby Elite, have inertia built in to the controller. When combined with a decoder that has inertia the result is a locomotive that takes ages to move, and to stop. In this situation you will want to amend the CVs that control the acceleration (CV 3) and deceleration (CV 4) rate on the locomotive decoder and set them to zero.

BELOW: Off at last. To get a good roar out of the loco, whack the controller up to full and then back off to the required speed as the train starts to move.

As the locomotive approaches its train you need to slow down in advance to a crawl and then set the controller to zero so that the locomotive gently slides up to its train. Hit F5 for the buffer clang (and then hit it again to reset the function). Assuming you are using tension locks, or other automatic couplings, you could start away immediately, but that doesn't mimic real life. A shunter would have to couple the locomotive to the train (press F6), couple up the brake pipes on a fitted freight or passenger train and the driver would have to perform a brake test (press F4). Right, now you're ready to start.

BOTTOM: Once under the bridge we will be on the hidden trackage and can silence the locomotive by pressing F1.

Change the direction on the controller and turn it up to a reasonable speed for travel within station limits. (Did you remember to give a quick blast on the horn before moving off?). Then when you are on the main line open the controller up. If you want to simulate the hard work needed to get a heavy train moving you should open the controller to full power and then throttle back when the train gets to the speed that you want. This will simulate the locomotive working under full load with the regulator wide open.

BELOW: Before the train emerges from behind a building onto the visible trackage we hit F1 again to restore the sound.

BOTTOM: We sound the two-tone horn as we pass the yard whilst the locomotive emits the characteristic Class 20 whistling sound.

On many layouts there are hidden tracks, often serving a fiddle yard. You really don't want sound coming out of trains in these locations, and certainly don't want to go through the start up or shut down procedures either. If you press F1 whilst the locomotive is in motion the sound will be turned on or off immediately. Ideally it would fade in or out, but on or off is better than nothing. Once the train disappears from view press F1 and everything will go quiet until you press F1 again, just before it reappears from the hidden trackage. As you approach a station at speed, trackside workers or anywhere that sounding your horn might seem a good idea you can give the familiar two-tone blast by pressing F3.

As I mentioned earlier, stopping at a precise spot when you are using the inertia function can be tricky. Over-running can be embarrassing, especially if you end up colliding with other stock or the buffers. You can use the shunting speed F7 to help here. As you approach the stop press F7. The locomotive will decelerate to half its previous speed and crawl. Now press F8 and you have direct control so you can stop on the proverbial sixpence. You can use F4 for the noise of the loco's air brake just before hitting F7 and again before you come to a halt.

The shunter can disconnect the brake pipes and uncouple the train, then you can potter off back to your quiet siding. Make sure the locomotive is stationary before you press F1 and the decoder will go through the shut down procedure. That's it, shift over.

One thing you will find is that as supplied, the volume is set rather loud, and the effect quickly becomes wearing on the ears. You can reduce the volume by changing the setting in CV63. As supplied it is set to the maximum volume (64). The ideal setting for your layout will depend on how noisy the locomotive is when

running. Shuttling back and forth along a 6' long shunting layout will be quieter than going full-tilt around a large circuit. The sound should be audible above, and mask the sound of, the locomotive's mechanism. On a continuous run I found that half volume (32) was a good compromise; for a shunting layout the value could go as low as a quarter (16). Don't make it too loud as if you have a number of sound locomotives in operation you'll have the neighbours round to complain!

Glossary

A (Amp)	A measure of electric current.
AC (Alternating current)	Electric current that constantly changes direction.
Accessory Decoder	A *decoder* that operates accessories such as points and signals rather than a locomotive.
Address	The number of a locomotive, comparable to a telephone number.
Analogue controller	Standard 12V *DC* controller, not capable of generating *DCC* commands.
Analogue locomotive	Standard 12V *DC* locomotive, not fitted with a *DCC decoder*.
Binary Number	A number made up of *bits*. Values count up in twos rather than 10s. So 1 represents 1, 10 represents 2, 100 represents 4, 1000 represents 8, and so on.
Bit	Short for BINARY DIGIT. A single value of 0 or 1. A single bit can be used to indicate if something is off or on. A number of bits can be used to make a *binary number*.
Booster	Takes the low power digital signal from the *command station* and amplifies it so that it has enough power to operate locomotives and accessories. A layout may have a number of boosters in order to provide sufficient power.
Bus	Wires used to distribute power and/or information around the layout.
Cab	Unit that allows you to set the speed and direction of a locomotive. May also provide other facilities such as control of *functions* and *programming*.
Command Station	The "brains" of the system. Takes information from the *cabs*, formats it for *DCC* operation and passes it as a digital signal to the *booster*.
Configuration Variable (CV)	*Address*, starting voltage, acceleration rate and deceleration rate are examples of features which can be customized within the locomotive *decoder*.
Consist	Method of controlling several locomotives at the same time with a common *address*
DC (Direct current)	Electric current that runs continuously in one direction.
DCC	Abbreviation for Digital Command Control
Decoder	A device that receives *DCC* commands and acts on them, for example to turn on a light or increase motor speed.
Extended Address/ Extended Addressing	Not supported by all command stations or decoders. This is a method that allows locomotive addresses from 128 to 9999 to be used.
Function	A *decoder* controlled switch that can be used to operate lights and other accessories.
Locomotive address	see *Address*
NMRA	National Model Railroad Association, North American model railroaders organization who control the *DCC* standards.
Programming	The process of setting the *Configuration Variables* of a *decoder*.
Programming on the main	The ability to set *Configuration Variables* of *decoders* whilst on the layout.
Programming track	A section of track, electrically isolated from the layout, used for setting and reading the *Configuration Variables* of a *decoder*.
Speed steps	The number of increments that a *decoder* uses to change from stop to full speed.
Walkaround controller	A handheld *cab* that allows the operator to move around with the locomotive that they are operating.

Troubleshooting Guide

Unable to program or read any decoders – System returns 'not found/incorrectly connected' error...

- Your wiring between the booster and programming track has too high a resistance – probably due to a bad connection or soldered joint. You can confirm this by running wires straight from the booster unit to the programming track and attaching direct to the rails using crocodile clips.

Can run analogue (DC) locomotives but DCC installed locomotives do not respond...

- Your wiring between the booster and layout has too high a resistance – probably due to a bad connection or soldered joint. You can confirm this by running wires straight from the booster unit to a length of track and attaching direct to the rails using crocodile clips.

All trains stop / The controller keeps on cutting out...

- There is a short circuit somewhere. Have you run a locomotive up to a point that is set against it? If you can isolate sections of your layout do so to try to locate it.
  Remove the locomotives one by one to see if any of them are causing the short circuit.
- The railway is taking more power than the system can supply. Reduce the number of locomotives and accessories in use. If this cures the problem then you need to install one or more booster units.

One locomotive will not respond to the controller...

Locomotives won't respond at all
- Check that you are using the correct decoder address!
- Check that there is power to the track.
  For example is the locomotive in a siding that has been isolated by a power routing point?
- Check that the short/long address bit is set correctly in the basic configuration register (CV 29)
- Check that no wires have come loose in the locomotive.
- The system is set for 128-speed step operation and the decoder does not support this mode.
- If you have changed a CV setting since the locomotive last worked – change it back.
- If all else fails reset the decoder – see the decoder instructions for how to reset it to the default settings.

Locomotives just stopped and now won't respond...
- Is the track dirty?
- The decoder might have overheated.
  Remove the locomotive from the track and let it cool down before trying to run the locomotive again.

The headlight and other functions are controllable but it won't run...

- This sometimes happens when you clear a consist but for some reason the decoder misses the command. Set CV19 to 0 to clear the consist information
- Check that the short/long address bit is set correctly in the basic configuration register (CV 29)

The headlight won't switch on...
- The command station and decoder are in different speed step modes.
- Is the headlight wired to the correct function output?
- Has the headlight bulb blown?

All locomotives behave oddly...

Locomotives run erratically...
- Clean track thoroughly

Some or all locomotives will not respond to the controller...
- Check that all the booster stations are turned on.

All locos stop responding to the controller...
- Turn the controller off. Wait a little while then turn it back on again.

One locomotive is behaving oddly...

Locomotives runs erratically...
- Clean locomotive wheels thoroughly and clean all electrical pickups.

Locomotives travels in the wrong direction.
- Wires to the motor brushes in the locomotive have been reversed. This can be corrected, without rewiring the loco, by setting bit 0 of the basic configuration register (CV 29) to 1.

Locomotives does not respond to function key.
- Try again. The locomotive may have been on dirty track and did not receive the command.
- Is that function valid for that locomotive and decoder?
- Check that no wires have come loose in the locomotive.

Head light goes on and off as it changes speed.
- You are operating a locomotive with an older 14-step decoder in the 28-step mode.

Head light goes off.
- Decoder has temporarily lost power and has reset itself.
- Clean track, locomotive wheels and electrical pickups.

Locomotive won't run on an analogue (DC) layout

- Check that the DC mode bit is set in the basic configuration register (CV 29).

Manufacturers and Suppliers (UK)

A&H Models
UK distributor of Lenz DCC equipment.
95 High Street
Brackley
NN13 7BW
Tel: 01280 701410
www.aandh-models.co.uk

Bachmann
Manufacturer of DCC equipment and models.
Moat Way
Barwell
LE9 8EY
www.bachmann.co.uk

Bromsgrove Models
Supplier of Hornby, Digitrax, ESU, MRC, NCE QSI, Soundtrax, TCS, Umelec and Zimo DCC equipment.
13 Fairmont Road
Bromsgrove
B60 2HJ
Mail/internet orders only.
Tel: 01527 877066
www.bromsgrovemodels.co.uk

DCC Supplies
Supplier of Digitrax, Hornby, ESU, Lenz, MRC, NCE QSI, Soundtrax, TCS and Zimo DCC equipment and ESU sound decoders with UK locomotive sounds.
Unit 17A Top Barn Business Centre
Worcester Road
Holt Heath
WR6 6NH
Tel: 0845 224 1601
www.dccsupplies.com

Express Models
Supplier of lighting kits.
65 Conway Drive
Shepshed
Loughborough
LE12 9PP
Tel: 01509 829008
Email:
sales@expressmodels.co.uk
www.expressmodels.co.uk

Gaugemaster
UK importer of MRC DCC equipment.
Gaugemaster House
Ford Road
Arundel
BN18 0BN
Tel: 01903 884321
www.gaugemaster.com

Hornby plc
Manufacturer of DCC equipment and models.
Westwood Industrial Estate
Margate
CT9 4JX
Tel: 01843 233535
www.hornby.com

Howes Models
Suppliers of ESU sound decoders with UK locomotive sounds.
12 Banbury Road
Kidlington
OX5 2BT
Tel: 01865 848000
www.howesmodels.co.uk

M G Sharp
Suppliers of Bachmann, Lenz, TCS, Digitrax, NCE & Roco DCC equipment.
712 Attercliffe Road
Sheffield
Tel: 0114 244 0851
www.mgsharp.com

Maplin Electronics Ltd.
Supplier of wire, electronic components, solder and tools. Stores nationwide.
Tel: 0870 4296000
www.maplin.co.uk

MERG/
Model Electronic Railway Group
Society for people interested in using electronics with model railways. Have their own range of self-build DCC items available as kits.
MERG Membership Secretary,
40 Compton Avenue
Poole
Dorset
BH14 8PY
www.merg.org.uk

Rapid Electronics Ltd.
Supplier of wire, electronic components, solder and tools.
Severalls Lane
Colchester
CO4 5JS
Tel: 01206 751166
www.rapidonline.com

South West Digital Ltd.
Supplier of ESU Lok-Sound decoders with UK locomotive sounds.
1 Savernake Road
Weston - Super - Mare
BS22 9HQ
Tel: 01934 517303
www.southwestdigital.co.uk

Sunningwell Command Control Ltd.
Supplier of Digitrax and Soundtrax DCC equipment.
PO Box 381
Abingdon
OX13 6YB
Tel/Fax: 01865 730455
www.scc4dcc.co.uk

Squires Model & Craft Tools
Supplier of wire, electronic components, solder and tools.
100 London Road
Bognor Regis
PO21 1DD
Tel: 01243 842424
Fax: 01243 842525